John Wright

Prodigious Political Ponderings & Prognostications...

-

...a sobering glance back; slouching into early Obama-nomics and Obamacare.

By John Wright

Published 2014 by John Wright

©2014 by John Wright

This book was printed in the United States by **CreateSpace;** (http://createspace.com/)

To order additional copies, contact **Createspace eStore.com/books**

ISBN-13: 978-1508642671
ISBN-10: 1508642672

Acknowledgements

To Ruth Rounds, Editor and Grammarian par excellence.
Gayle Maurer, the quintessential Graphic Artist.
Ray Hoy, whose incredible Formatting skills
made this book possible.

Table of Contents

2008	**Pg. 9**
2009	**Pg. 551**
2010	**Pg. 142**
2011	**Pg. 170**
2012-2013	**Pg. 194**

CadillaqJaq Examines The Issues

A "Flyover Country" Conservative takes a look at the numerous issues facing our nation in this less than satisfactory period.

"If I didn't change your mind, perhaps I at the least caused you to consider a different point of view."

John Wright~

Introduction

I recently found myself researching for a comment I wrote few years ago in a political blog I submitted on the Internet. While reading it, and a couple of others, I became aware that many of my opinions still had merit today, years later. The following is a partial collection of both Blogs and Letters to the Editor of my local newspaper. *(More would have been available, but for an HD crash one stormy night).*

Regardless of your political affiliation, if you have forgotten (or perhaps didn't know) how our nation got into the condition we find it today, maybe this will stimulate your recollection and give you some assistance in picking and choosing when you next visit the voting booth.

About the Author

My initial attempt at political opinion writing began in 1959 following the election of JFK, before his inauguration when I penned a Letter to the Editor of the Detroit Free Press suggesting that in a spirit of bipartisan-ship, President-elect Kennedy might ask Nixon's running mate, and former UN Ambassador Henry Cabot Lodge, to remain on in the United Nations. A couple of days later, comments supporting my suggestion filled the entire op-Ed page. I was overwhelmed. Those responses and a new Olivetti typewriter got me started.

In the years following, I wrote hundreds of Letters to the Editors from Michigan to Colorado to California. The vast majority of them were published and supporting comments were not a rarity. In the mid-1990s, I discovered the Internet and political chat rooms. On AOL, I ran into syndicated journalist Tony Snow, whose opinions appeared regularly in the Detroit Free Press. Later he worked for FOX Cable News, which ultimately led to his appointment as press secretary to President G.W. Bush.

Until then, Tony Snow and I exchanged dozens of emails and he gave me many valuable tips on political writing. I cherish those times and the emails we exchanged. Tony Snow was a really decent human being.

In 2006-7, while still voicing conservative political views on occasion, I had a "fun run" doing anecdotal blogs on <u>Sporting News.com</u> with a few dozen other amateur writers. Then this young fellow, Barack H. Obama, started making headlines as *the* new post-racial politician; a "Man of Change."

Using the pseudonym of 'CadillaqJaq' as a contributor to <u>Blogspot.com</u>, and <u>Blogs Lucianne Loves</u>, I attempted to listen to candidate Obama objectively, but there was something I couldn't put my finger on; something almost 'Nixonian' about him.

My biggest objection initially to Barack Obama as a presidential candidate was his lack of executive experience, especially to fill the job as Commander in Chief, that and he had no foreign affairs experience. His Cairo speech definitely convinced me I was right in that instance, but, as I am deign to say too often, 'being right and a dollar will get you marginal cup of coffee'.

In my blogs, I attempted to clarify my displeasure through the early years of his presidency. While formatting and preparing this book into paperback, I found myself reading some of my opinions from years back and was more than surprised how accurate some of my prognostications were. I guess even a 'blind squirrel finds an occasional acorn.'

So, as my blog banner says; "If I didn't change your mind, perhaps at the least I caused you to consider a different point of view."

Enjoy.

John Wright

<u>*2008*</u>

Friday, October 3, 2008
<u>Let's Clear the Air!</u>
by J. Wright

(My opinion piece was printed by the Cadillac (MI) News...

A good friend of mine, a staunch liberal, recently had a partial out-of-context remark published, credited to presidential candidate Senator John McCain regarding proposed health care deregulation that read, "… as we have done over the last decade in banking..." implying that this deregulation would give health care providers an unsupervised blank check. Not so.

Let's clear the air. Factcheck.org, an impartial Internet fact-finding group, stated that was a twisting of McCain's words referring to presidential candidate Barack Obama's recent ad using the same incomplete, out-of-context phrase.

Here's the full text of Senator John McCain's statement:
"I would also allow individuals to choose to purchase health insurance across state lines, when they can find more affordable and attractive products elsewhere that they prefer. Opening up the health insurance market to more vigorous nationwide competition, as we have done over the last decade in banking, would provide more choices of innovative products less burdened by the worst excesses of state-based regulation. Consumer-friendly insurance policies will be more available and affordable when there is greater competition among insurers on a level playing field. You should be able to buy your insurance from any willing provider—the state bureaucracies are no better than national ones. Nationwide insurance markets that ensure broad and vigorous competition will wring out excess costs, overhead, and bloated executive compensation."

As Factcheck.org also stated, "Note that McCain began by speaking of buying insurance 'across state lines.' His comparison with banking regulation was limited to 'opening up the insurance market' to 'nationwide' competition to 'provide more choices' to consumers."

Presidential candidate Barack Obama has claimed that words have meanings. I contend if we are to use other people's words, let's use their entire statement in order to clarify their original intent, not to confuse and scare the voters.

Thanks for your time, Jaq

Saturday, October 4, 2008

"Smokin' OPs..."

by J. Wright

OPs?

Yeah, remember when you smoked those nasty old cigarettes and discovered that you'd suddenly ran out? Next move; you borrowed one from a buddy. OP is an acronym for "Other Peoples." In this case I borrowed the title of this blog from a Bob Seger mid-1970s record album.

The article below is from:
(http://www.exposeobama.com/obamataxesbe.html)

It's a few weeks old: BLDEBO. *(Before Latest Disastrous Economic Bailout)*. It goes like this: "The Obama spend-o-meter is now up around $800-billion and tax hikes on the rich won't pay for it." *Lawrence Kudlow-*

Just to make it clearer, Mister Kudlow goes on: "It's the middle class that will ultimately shoulder this fiscal burden in terms of higher taxes and lower growth..." $800-billion... that's a staggering figure!

Just to put it in perspective, the United States government collected approximately $2.6-trillion in revenues in 2007. $800-billion is 30% of that figure! $800-billion would represent the GREATEST EXPANSION OF GOVERNMENT in the history of the United States!

To put it in further perspective, $800-billion is about $6.800.00 per household or $2,700.00 for every man, woman and child in the United States!

And YOU get to pay for it! Mister Kudlow lists just a few of Obama's goals:
- $150-billion on a green-energy plan.
- An infrastructure investment bank to the tune of $60-billion.
- An expansion of health insurance by roughly $65 billion. Steve Moore, writing for The Wall Street Journal did the math. The Weekly Standard quotes him as saying that Obama's tax proposals will add up to a "39.6% personal income tax, a 52.2% combined income and payroll tax, a 2% capital-gains tax, a 39.6% dividend tax and a 55% estate tax."

But What About Obama's Middle Class Tax Cut?
Isn't He Just Going To Take From The Rich? Make no mistake, Barack Hussein Obama WILL raise your taxes! He won't just raise taxes on the "rich." He'll raise YOUR TAXES! He'll raise your children's taxes. He'll raise your grandchildren's taxes! To paraphrase former-President Ronald Reagan, "If it moves, he WILL tax it!"

Let's take a real close at one of his middle-class tax relief proposals. According to <u>Politico.com</u>: "Sen. Barack Obama (D-Ill.) on Friday announced an 'Emergency Economic Plan' that would give families a stimulus check of $1,000 each, funded IN PART by what his presidential campaign calls 'windfall profits from Big Oil'.

Separately, Obama's plan includes a $50 billion stimulus package. Essentially, Obama wants to fund something on the order of $100-billion - $200-billion dollars a year on the back of Big Oil. But, we've been down this road before and history tells us what happens when we tax the "windfall profits" of oil companies. Tax revenues go DOWN to NOTHING and the domestic oil industry collapses!

Internet blogger Michelle Malkin recently quoted a Congressional Research Service (CRS) assessment of the Carter-era windfall profits tax:

"[T]he windfall profits tax was forecasted to raise more than $320-billion between 1980 and 1989. However, according to the CRS, the government collected only $80-billion in gross tax revenue ($146 billion in 2004 dollars). The net amount was actually less than this -- roughly $40-billion -- because the tax was deductible against corporate income."

"[T]he windfall profits tax was forecasted to raise more than $320-billion between 1980 and 1989. However, according to the CRS, the government collected only $80-billion in gross tax revenue ($146 billion in 2004 dollars). The net amount was actually less than this -- roughly $40-billion.

"CRS also found the windfall profits tax had the effect of decreasing domestic production by 3 percent to 6 percent, thereby increasing American dependence on foreign oil sources by 8 percent to 16 percent. A side effect was declining, not increasing, tax collections. Figure 1 clearly shows that while the tax raised considerable revenue in the initial years following its enactment, those revenues declined to almost nothing as the domestic industry collapsed."

So, who is going to pay for President Barack Hussein Obama's grand income redistribution scheme? You can be certain of this much... that $1000.00 check will come in handy -- if it ever comes -- particularly when the price of gasoline at the pump goes up even further, the taxes collected from the oil companies drops to 'nada', and Obama searches for other sources of revenue to make up the difference!

Who Is Going To Pay For All This?

According to Obama's campaign website:

"Barack Obama is the only candidate who has a real middle class relief plan. He will provide $1,000 in a refundable tax credit to working families, create a universal mortgage interest credit for homeowners who can't benefit from a mortgage tax incentive available to wealthier Americans, and create a $4,000 college tax credit for middle class families."

"Obama will eliminate all income taxation of seniors making less than $50,000 per year. This will provide an immediate tax cut averaging $1,400 to 7-million seniors and relieve millions from the burden of filing tax returns."

$1,400.00 times 7-million... That's $9.8 billion. A $1,000 tax credit and a $4,000 college tuition credit... we're talking hundreds of billion of dollars!

Again, who is going to pay for all of this? YOU ARE! That is, if it happens at all...

Remember what happened the last time a Democrat running for president promised a middle-class tax cut? In his very first campaign ad, which aired in January of 1992, Bill Clinton stated: *"I'm Bill Clinton and I believe that you deserve more than 30-second ads and vague promises. That's why I've offered a comprehensive plan to get our economy moving again, to take care of our own people, and regain our economic leadership. It starts with a tax cut for the middle class and asks the rich to pay their fair share."*

Within days of taking office, Clinton reneged on that promise. On nationwide television, he said he, 'tried as hard as he could' but just couldn't deliver! At least he 'felt our pain'. You could see the heartfelt agony in his face over breaking that promise! Then, it only took him about TWO MONTHS to push the largest tax increase in United States history on the American people through Congress! It was one of his top priorities! And like Bill Clinton, Barack Hussein Obama was never shy about taxes.

At the Democratic Presidential Debate at Howard University on June 28, 2007, Obama said: *"And the Bush tax cuts--people didn't need them, and they weren't even asking for them, and that's why they need to be less, so that we can pay for universal health care and other initiatives."*

In his response to the 2008 State of the Union Address, Obama stated: *"[W]e know that at a time of war and economic hardship, the last thing we need is a permanent tax cut for Americans who don't need them and weren't even asking for them."*

When questioned on the issue of taxes at the Democratic Presidential Debate in Los Angeles, California on January 30, 2008, Obama proudly boasted: *"I'm not bashful about it."*

A middle-class tax cut? It won't happen!

If we're lucky, Barack Hussein Obama will give with one hand and take (a greater amount) with the other! 'Obama giveth and Obama taketh away' (after all, some have called him a "Messiah").

That's why we call it, 'income redistribution!' Giving Your Money To The World... But Obama's income redistribution schemes doesn't stop at the shores of the United States! Let us not forget Barack Hussein Obama's Global Poverty Act -- a bill that lays the groundwork for -- according to some estimates -- what could amount to a $845-billion United Nations tax on the people of the United States!

And just how much is $845-billion? Vincent Gioia, writing in Right Side News, translates this incomprehensible figure into language every American understands: "This amounts to a tax of over $2,000 on each man, woman and child in the United States. The foreign aid budget now stands at $300 billion; the Act would add the additional expenditure to the already huge amount allocated to assist the world."

But wait a minute, folks! The Global Poverty Act is part of a much larger United Nations scheme. The United Nations' Millennium Development Goal -- proclaimed in 2000 -- contains plans for the additional plundering of your bank account. Among their stated goals are: · a "currency transfer tax", -- that is, a tax imposed on companies and individuals who, in the course of traveling or doing international business, must exchange dollars for foreign currency;

- *a tax on the rental value of land and natural resources;*
- *and fees for the commercial use of the oceans,*
- *fees for airplanes use of the skies,*
- *fees for the use of the electromagnetic spectrum...*
- *and a tax on the carbon content of fuels.*

NOW is the time to take the fight to Senator Barack Hussein Obama and Speaker of the House Nancy Pelosi and Senate Majority Leader Harry Reid.

NOW is the time to make it clear to the American people that Obama, Pelosi and Reid stand for higher taxes and more failed socialist programs that will squeeze the wealth from middle-class Americans and that we stand for lower taxes and personal prosperity.

Demand that they push the issue NOW!

Demand that they dare Barack Hussein Obama and Nancy Pelosi and Harry Reid to oppose them and, in the process, force Obama, Pelosi and Reid to show their true tax-and-spend colors to the American people!

In about 30 days we will elect the next President of the United States. That's not a lot of time and there is not a moment to lose!

Thanks for your time, Jaq

Sunday, October 5, 2008

Don't Blame the Republicans for the Bailout's Failure or its Cause!

by J. Wright

(This opinion piece of mine was printed in the Cadillac, MI, News on Tuesday, September 30, 2008)

A bit more than 30 minutes into a 15-minute vote Monday in the U.S. House of Representatives it became apparent that nearly 100 Democrats voting in tandem with more than 130 Republicans had heard the loud voices of their constituents and voted against a $700-billion taxpayer funded bailout of financial institutions that previously made questionable mortgage loans to questionable applicants, all in the guise of "affordable housing."

Following the vote, Speaker of the House Nancy Pelosi, D-CA, found the TV cameras and proceeded to blame the failure of the legislation on the House Republicans, conveniently forgetting that her Democrats have a majority of the votes in the House and could have easily passed it without any Republican votes.

What she also forgot were basic social graces; if you seek bipartisanship don't poison a session prior to an important vote with a starkly partisan speech, hammering your opponents then expect their cooperation.

As far as blame for this entire financial mess, it's my opinion that its roots go back to 1977 when Democrat President Jimmy Carter signed the Community Reinvestment Act (CRA) into law. CRA prohibited lending institutions from "redlining" or discriminating against neighborhoods, in particular, high financial risk neighborhoods.

With those restrictions removed, Pandora's Box was opened to allow financial institutions to make questionable real estate loans, which coincidentally seems to be the biggest economic problem today.

Many institutions that refused to abide by CRA were threatened with federal lawsuit if they didn't comply and make the questionable loans. Protesters from the political action groups such as ACORN and the SEIU overran the lobbies of some banks. Only in Socialist America?

So where does the real blame fall? On the 1977 Congress that enacted the CRA legislation? Certainly not on today's Congress... this Democrat controlled Congress is seemingly "without sin." Ask any of them.

Today, in this era of overblown partisan bickering, President George W. Bush and the Republicans are labeled the fall guys. Following him, it's presidential contender Senator John McCain, R-AZ.

Someone please tell me how anyone in their right mind can agree with that premise, especially when it was Senator McCain in 2005 and George W. Bush later, warning the country of the impending crisis featuring Fannie Mae and Freddie Mac, and then McCain was ridiculed by his Democrat Senate associates?

Go online and find anything that Democrats Senator Christopher Dodd or Representative Barney Frank said in warning of their collapse. No, all you will find are positive statements about how strong the two agencies are. It's pretty damning when you actually read their words.

For further evidence, please check out this link to a video filmed in the U.S. House, a C-Span filmed video of Democrat Representatives covering up the Fannie Mae, Freddie Mac Scam that caused our current Economic Crisis... unless you are willing to discount what your eyes and ears tell you.

http://www.youtube.com/watch?v=_MGT_cSi7Rs&feature=email

Thanks for your time, Jaq

Monday, October 6, 2008

Obama's Campaign Contributions In Doubt...

by J. Wright

Mike Isikopff, veteran Newsweek columnist, files in his latest column: "The Obama campaign has shattered all fund-raising records, raking in $458 million so far, with about half the bounty coming from donors who contribute $200 or less. Aides say that's an illustration of a truly democratic campaign. To critics, though, it can be an invitation for fraud and illegal foreign cash because donors giving individual sums of $200 or less don't have to be publicly reported.

For the complete article: http://www.newsweek.com/id/162403

As most of you are aware, Newsweek is NOT a flaming right-wing publication, so when they become alarmed that all is not on the up-and-up in Obama-land, maybe it's time for the voters to take note.

In the past couple of weeks, I have read a couple of other articles seriously questioning Obama's campaign sources. $458-million or so is a bundle of cash in which to keep an accurate accounting. His staff claims that about half of it came from small contributions of less than $200 each from hundreds of thousands of contributors. They go on to claim that that's proof of his vast popularity. But, some of it came from foreign sources, including the Hamas terrorist controlled Gaza Strip bordering Israel, and that folks is illegal. One article I read says that about $200-million of the funds raised are in question. His campaign returned a few thousand dollars; much, much more was not. Does the average voter care? I'd say the average voter isn't even aware.

Quoting from Isikopff's article, "Some critics say the campaign hasn't done enough. This summer, watchdog groups asked both campaigns to share more information about its small donors. The McCain campaign agreed; the Obama campaign did not. They could've done themselves a service by heeding the suggestions, said Massie Ritsch of the Center for Responsive Politics.

Will the tepid Republican National Committee, who is now suing for disclosure and for alleged violation of campaign contribution laws, or the Federal Election Committee have time to get the real facts before the election? You'd have to be delirious to believe that will happen. Campaign contribution laws and regulations are broken all the time, but no one pays the price until it's too late, usually after the offending party is happily ensconced in office and out of harm's way. Pitiful.

Thanks for your time, Jaq

Monday, October 6, 2008

Where did the Money Come From?

by J. Wright

This is from an email forwarded to me by Cal; an old friend and former employment supervisor, apparently emailed to him and signed by someone named "Stan".

I have no way to prove or disprove the veracity of its contents.

Dear Calvin,

This election has me very worried. So many things to consider. About a year ago, I would have voted for Obama. I have changed my mind three times since then. I watch all the news channels, jumping from one to another. I must say this drives me crazy. However, I feel if you view MSNBC, CNN, and Fox News, you might get some middle ground with which to work.

About six months ago, I started thinking, "Where did the money come from for Obama". I have four daughters who went to College, we were middle class, and money was tight. We (including my girls) worked hard and there were many student loans. I started looking into Obama's life.

Around 1979 Obama started college at Occidental in California. He is very open about his two years at Occidental, he tried all kinds of drugs and was wasting his time but, even though he had a brilliant mind, did not apply himself to his studies. "Barry" (that was the name he used all his life) during this time had two roommates, Muhammad Hasan Chandoo and Wahid Hamid, both from Pakistan.

During the summer of 1981, after his second year in college, he made a "round the world" trip. Stopping to see his mother in Indonesia, next Hyderabad in India, three weeks in Karachi, Pakistan, where he stayed with his roommate's family, then off to Africa to visit his father's family. My question - Where did he get the money for this trip?

Nether I, nor any one of my children would have had money for a trip like this when they were in college. When he came back, he started school at Columbia University in New York. It is at this time he wants everyone to call him Barack - not Barry. Do you know what the tuition is at Columbia? It's not cheap to say the least! Where did he get money for tuition? Student Loans? Maybe.

After Columbia, he went to Chicago to work as a Community Organizer for $12,000 a year. Why Chicago? Why not New York? He was already living in New York. By "chance", he met Antoin "Tony" Rezko, born in Aleppo, Syria, and a real estate developer in Chicago. Rezko has been convicted of fraud and bribery this year. Rezko, was named "Entrepreneur of the Decade" by the Arab-American Business and Professional Association.

About two years later, Obama entered Harvard Law School. Do you have any idea what tuition is for Harvard Law School? Where did he get the money for Law School? More student loans? After Law school, he went back to Chicago. Rezko offered him a job, which he turned down. However, he did take a job with Davis, Miner, Barnhill & Galland. Guess what? They represented "Rezar" which is Rezko's firm. Rezko was one of Obama's first major financial contributors when he ran for office in Chicago. In 2003, Rezko threw an early fundraiser for Obama which Chicago Tribune reporter David Mendelland claims was instrumental in providing Obama with "seed money" for his U.S. Senate race.

In 2005, Obama purchased a new home in Kenwoood District of Chicago for $1.65 million (less than asking price). With ALL those Student Loans, where did he get the money for the property? On the same day Rezko's wife, Rita, purchased the adjoining empty lot for full price. The London Times reported that Nadhmi Auchi, an Iraqi-born Billionaire loaned Rezko $3.5 million three weeks before Obama's new home was purchased. Obama met Nadhmi Auchi many times with Rezko. Now, we have Obama running for President.

Valerie Jarrett, was Michele Obama's boss. She is now Obama's chief advisor and he does not make any major decisions without talking to her first. Where was Jarrett born? Ready for this? Shiraz, Iran! Do we see a pattern here? On the other hand, am I going crazy?

On May 10, 2008 The Times reported, Robert Malley advisor to Obama was "sacked" after the press found out he was having regular contacts with "Hamas", which controls Gaza and is connected with Iran. This past week, buried in the back part of the newspapers, Iraqi papers reported that during Obama's visit to Iraq, he asked their leaders to do nothing about the war until after he is elected and he will "Take care of things". Oh, and by the way, remember the college roommates that where born in Pakistan? They are in charge of all those "small" Internet campaign contributions for Obama.

Where is that money coming from? The poor and middle class in this country? Or could it be from the Middle East? And the final bit of news. On September 7, 2008, The Washington Times posted a verbal slip Obama made on This Week with George Stephanopoulos.

Obama on talking about his religion said, "My Muslim faith". When questioned, "...he made a mistake". Some mistake!

All of the above information I got on line. If you would like to check it - visit Wikipedia encyclopedia, search: Barack Obama; Tony Rezko; Valerie Jarrett: Daily Times.

Obama visited Pakistan in 1981; The Washington Times –September 7, 2008; The Times May 10, 2008.

Now the BIG question - If I found out all this information on my own, why haven't all of our "intelligent" members of the press been reporting this? A phrase that keeps ringing in my ear – "Beware of the enemy from within!"

P.S. Cal, I checked most of this info out myself and it is factual!

Stan

... ...

As I said at the beginning, I received a forwarded copy of this email a week ago from an old friend and former supervisor it was signed by *Stan*. My former supervisor's name is NOT Stan so I'm certain he didn't generate it, he merely passed it along for my consumption.

The questions posed by its author are valid; we don't know jack-shit about Obama *(or his campaign contributions that are under some scrutiny now by the FEC)* other than as John McCain finally admitted, Obama came out of nowhere and hasn't done much of anything since except run for the highest office in the land and write two autobiographies. That act of *running for office*, in Obama's own words, is qualification enough that he has the basic executive experience to *run the country*. Oh, really? I use 'run' loosely as most presidents are flummoxed by a contrary Congress and don't accomplish a fraction of what they set out to do, ergo their campaign promises are a joke.

Back to experience: I've watched TVs <u>Law & Order</u> series from its outset, and, for many more years than Barack Obama has been in the U.S. Senate... I suppose that qualifies me run for the office County

Prosecutor here in northern Michigan's beautiful Wexford County. Damn, it's too late to get on this election ballot, so I'd better get busy writing a couple of autobiographies in order to settle in on exactly who I am and what I might be about.

There is this little unresolved problem of qualifications... in order to serve as president of the United States, one must be born in the United States or one of its protectorates, as explained here, to wit:

Qualifications for the Office of President
Age and Citizenship requirements - US Constitution, Article II, Section

No person except a natural born citizen, or a citizen of the United States, at the time of the adoption of this Constitution, shall be eligible to the office of President; neither shall any person be eligible to that office who shall not have attained to the age of thirty-five years, and been fourteen years a resident within the United States.

Term limit amendment - US Constitution, Amendment XXII, Section 1 – ratified February 27, 1951

No person shall be elected to the office of the President more than twice, and no person who has held the office of President, or acted as President, for more than two years of a term to which some other person was elected President shall be elected to the office of the President more than once.

So our liberal friends and others will continue to argue about what the definition of the word "is" is... and they will pathetically argue as to what the Founding Fathers meant by "natural born," as in one such remark, *"Duh, does that mean born without the use of an anesthetic painkiller, man?"*

In a case now pending, Barack Obama and his legal counsel, instead of producing a valid birth certificate, chose instead to fend off a pending legal action taken in Pennsylvania by a Phillip J. Berg, attorney-at-law, who is petitioning the presiding court to force Obama to produce such a document, if there is such a thing. Instead, this is the latest response:

Lafayette Hill, Pennsylvania – 09/24/08
Philip J. Berg, Esquire, the Attorney who filed suit against Barack H. Obama challenging Senator Obama's lack of "qualifications" to serve as President of the United States, announced today that Obama and Democratic National Committee [DNC] filed a Joint Motion-to-Dismiss on the last day, to file a response, for the obvious purpose of delaying Court action in the case of Berg v. Obama, No. 08-CV-04083.

Their joint motion indicates a concerted effort to avoid the truth by delaying the judicial process, although legal, by not resolving the issue presented: that is, whether Barack Obama was "natural born."

So many questions, so little time. Later ... take care out there.

Thanks for your time, Jaq

Wednesday, October 8, 2008
Causality; Coincidence; Casualty...
by J. Wright

Causality; Coincidence; Casualty . . . three words that in most cases have no connection. Unless they do.

Anymore I follow the stock market only to the point of determining if the Dow-Jones average went up today or dropped. I'm not an investor any more. My history of investing is similar to my history as a poker player; I'm not very good at either. You can't get ahead by breaking even so I avoid both the market and the card game.

I do watch political trends as many in the market do and I see one now. That's where *Causality* may be in play. Since Treasury Secretary Paulson and President Bush proclaimed that we needed a $700-billion bailout of Wall Street, presidential candidate Obama's poll ratings have been creeping ever higher. Conversely, the stock market has not. We've seen record losses almost on a daily basis. Is it a *Coincidence,* or is there more to it? The dreaded cause and effect factor?

Do the market investors see in Obama something that is worrisome? Frankly, I do, based on both he and his running mate's avoidance in answering a simple question: which of your proposed spending programs would you drop or cut? Both Obama and Biden have successfully avoided naming any, instead they ramble on about the importance of the programs they will keep, most of them requiring huge increases in spending, spending tax dollars that aren't there. Give Senator McCain some credit-- at least twice now he has said he would enact a spending freeze except for defense and veterans affairs.

Casualties, the third word I listed might come into play with an Obama presidency. Though Obama would seek to build a new economy from the "bottom up," there's no way that unfortunate economic times will not affect those at the bottom.

Thanks for your time, Jaq

Thursday, October 16, 2008

<u>Really, who is he?</u>

by J. Wright

One positive thing that Senator John McCain can claim, regardless of the outcome of the upcoming election; he exonerated former Senator Robert Dole, who previously ran the most inept campaign in Republican Party history.

John "Maverick" McCain is not one of my favorites, as I posted here months ago, but at least he is a known quantity as opposed to his Democrat opponent, Senator Barack H. Obama.

Barack Obama is a "new kid on the block" politically, finishing his fourth year in the U.S. Senate, where he spent less than 150 actual days on the job, the balance of the time running for our highest office. Before that, he was an Illinois State Senator. Cool, calm and collected, he reads well from a TelePrompTer in front of large audiences. As one critic remarked, 'In that capacity, he does as good a job as the average television news anchor.' And with this vast accumulation of qualifications, he could become our next president?

His accomplishments are few, his record is sparse. He did author two autobiographies, apparently to get it right as to who he is. But, who is he? To many of us he's a totally unknown quantity, but with the incredible capability to attract huge amounts of campaign cash in small quantities, some from questionable Internet subscribers with no vowels in their names or addresses.

To many of his followers and supporters, he is akin to being Messianic, one who at the campaign's beginning advocated 'Change,' but nearing the end he comes off as just another liberal tax and spend politician; ask "Joe the Plumber." A young politician with questionable past associates, who if connected to John McCain would have driven him from the race early on.

Obviously, the power of the biased media is in full bloom today; it successfully handpicked McCain, the weakest of the Republican field, and they certainly picked Barack Obama. Trick 'em, vote for McCain.

Thanks for your time, Jaq

Friday, October 17, 2008
Obama and "distribution of the wealth."
by J. Wright

So, the Democratic presidential contender, Barack Obama, wants to "redistribute the wealth." At least that's what he let slip last week while chatting with Ohioan, Joe Wurzelbacher, the plumber. Unfortunately the live TV cameras recorded his very words. How very arrogant of him; how very Socialist of him . . . and all of my life I thought we lived in a Free Enterprise society where you were taxed fairly on what you earned and encouraged to prosper and attain the American Dream.

Apparently, Obama has a different slant on what constitutes the American Dream. Can it be that the encroaching liberal "entitlement attitude" has jaded his thinking? That no one should enjoy an abundance of success, which in most cases means accumulating wealth? That in the best class warfare scenario its "unfair" to succeed while others have not?

This could be the biggest gaffe in Obama's short political career. It's my opinion that most Americans would not favor any socialist plan to "redistribute their wealth." Especially at the expense of being taxed at a greater rate. Believe what you will, at some point the existing Bush tax cuts will expire soon and guess what? The Harry Reid-Nancy Pelosi led Democrats in Washington, D.C. are perfectly willing to let them expire, allowing the tax rates to return to the higher levels of the Clinton years. Yet, they refuse to call that a tax increase. What would you call it? Change?

If you as the voters are willing to elect an individual whose philosophy is to take from the rich and give to the poor as Obama's proposing in his so-called middle class tax cut plan where of the 95% whose taxes will be lowered includes 30-40% who do NOT pay any tax at all, will receive a "welfare" check labeled a "tax credit" from Uncle Sam (taxpayer's dollars) then he's your man.

Thanks for your time, Jaq~

Monday, October 20, 2008

Joe Biden's scary prediction...

by J. Wright

How quickly the balance on the political stage shifts ... last week it was "Senator Government," aka Senator Barack Obama, inadvertently saying he wanted to "...just spread the wealth around." A very Marxist/Socialist un-American philosophy to take from the advantaged and 'spread' around to the disadvantaged.

On Monday, "Senator Gaffe," aka Senator Joe Biden, Obama's vice-presidential choice spoke, unaware there were media types present Biden said to a roomful of donors, *"Mark my words. It will not be six months before the world tests Barack Obama like they did John Kennedy."*

He continued, *"The world is looking. We're about to elect a brilliant 47-year-old senator president of the United States of America. Remember I said it standing here, if you don't remember anything else I said,"* Biden continued. *"Watch, we're going to have an international crisis, a generated crisis, to test the mettle of this guy."*

That "guy" Senator Biden referred to is none other than Senator Barack Obama, perhaps the next president of the United States. Unless the voters take a good look at the 'brilliant 47-year old senator' who Joe Biden himself criticized earlier during the Democratic primaries, saying Obama was unprepared to become the chief executive, adding that 'the Oval Office is not a place for on-the-job training.'

Afterward, the McCain camp released this statement: *"There has been no harsher critic of Barack Obama's lack of experience than Joe Biden. Biden has denounced Barack Obama's poor foreign policy judgment and has strongly argued in his own words what Americans are quickly realizing -- that Barack Obama is not ready to be President."*

Obviously, the McCain camp is biased, but really, is Obama ready to be the next president? That's for the voters to decide. While Biden's prediction is scary, would he say the same if McCain were elected?

Thanks for your time, Jaq

Wednesday, October 22, 2008

Another "OP"

by J. Wright

*(. . . **OP** stands for "**Other Peoples**")* This is a great one too, kiddies, written by Orson Scott Card; Pulitzer Prize material in my opinion. J. Wright

Would the Last Honest Reporter Please Turn On the Lights?
By Orson Scott Card--

Editor's note: Orson Scott Card is a <u>Democrat and a newspaper columnist</u>. In this opinion piece, he takes on both entities while lamenting the current state of journalism.

An open letter to the local daily paper — almost every local daily paper in America: I remember reading <u>All the President's Men</u> and thinking:

That's journalism. You do what it takes to get the truth and you lay it before the public, because the public has a right to know.

This housing crisis didn't come out of nowhere. It was not a vague emanation of the evil Bush administration.

It was a direct result of the political decision, back in the late 1990s, to loosen the rules of lending so that home loans would be more accessible to poor people. Fannie Mae and Freddie Mac had the authorization to approve risky loans.

(Jaq's Note: Are you familiar with a bill called the Community Reinvestment Act [CRA] passed and signed into law by President Jimmy Carter in 1977? The CRA prohibited financial institutions from using their previous "Red Line" qualifying process that identified questionable real estate neighborhoods and forced them [Under threat of federal lawsuit in some cases)to make questionable loans to questionable applicants. Read: bad or risky loans]. All of this with the approval of the Democrat led Congress; then and now.)

What is a risky loan anyway? Um … maybe it's a loan that the recipient is not likely able to repay.

The goal of this rule change was to 'help the poor' — which especially would help members of minority groups. But how does it help these people to give them a loan that they can't repay? They get into a house, yes, but when they can't make the payments, they lose the house — along with their credit rating. They end up worse off than before.

This was completely foreseeable and in fact many people did foresee it. One political party, in Congress and in the executive branch, tried repeatedly to tighten up the rules. The other party blocked every such attempt and tried to loosen them. *(To pander to a particular voting bloc?)*

Furthermore, Freddie Mac and Fannie Mae were making political contributions to the very members of Congress who were allowing them to make irresponsible loans. *(Though why quasi-federal agencies were granted the powwer to do so baffles me. It's kin to allowing the Pentagon to contribute to the political campaigns of Congressmen who support increasing their budget.)*

(Jaq's note: For certain, it seems, no Legislator is going to hamper his or her ability to raise campaign funds, ensuring themselves a longer stay at the public trough, slopping like the pigs many of them are.)

Isn't there a story here? Doesn't journalism require that you who produce our daily paper tell the truth about who brought us to a position where the only way to keep confidence in our economy was a $700 billion bailout? Aren't you supposed to follow the money and see which politicians were benefiting personally from the deregulation of mortgage lending?

I have no doubt that if these facts had pointed to the Republican Party or to John McCain as the guilty parties, you would be treating it as a vast scandal. "Housing-gate," no doubt. Or "Fannie-gate." Instead, it was Senator Christopher Dodd and Congressman Barney Frank, both Democrats, who denied that there were any problems, who refused Bush administration requests to set up a regulatory agency to watch over Fannie Mae and Freddie Mac, and who were still pushing for these agencies to go even further in promoting sub-prime mortgage loans almost up to the minute they failed.

As reputable journalist Thomas Sowell points out in a TownHall.com essay entitled Do Facts Matter? *(http://snipurl.com/457townhall_com)*

Alan Greenspan warned them four years ago. So did the Chairman of the Council of Economic Advisers to the President. So did Bush's Secretary of the Treasury.

These are facts. This financial crisis was completely preventable. The party that blocked any attempt to prevent it was … the Democratic Party. The party that tried to prevent it was … the Republican Party.

Yet when Nancy Pelosi accused the Bush administration and Republican deregulation of causing the crisis, you in the press did not hold her to account for her lie. Instead, you criticized Republicans who took offense at this lie and refused to vote for the bailout!

What? It's not the liar, but the victims of the lie who are to blame?

Now let's follow the money … right to the presidential candidate who is the number-two recipient of campaign contributions from Fannie Mae.

And after Franklin Raines, the CEO of Fannie Mae who made $90 million while running it into the ground, was fired for his incompetence, one presidential candidate's campaign actually *consulted him for advice on housing.*

If that presidential candidate had been John McCain, you would have called it a major scandal and we would be getting stories in your paper every day about how incompetent and corrupt he was.

But instead, that candidate was Barack Obama, and so you have buried this story, and when the McCain campaign dared to call Raines an "adviser" to the Obama campaign — because that campaign had sought his advice — you actually let Obama's people get away with accusing McCain of lying, merely because Raines wasn't listed as an official adviser to the Obama campaign. You would never tolerate such weasely nit-picking from a Republican.

If you who produce our local daily paper actually had any principles, you would be pounding this story, because the prosperity of all Americans was put at risk by the foolish, shortsighted, politically selfish, and possibly corrupt actions of leading Democrats, including Obama.

If you who produce our local daily paper had any personal honor, you would find it unbearable to let the American people believe that somehow Republicans were to blame for this crisis.

There are precedents. Even though President Bush and his administration never said that Iraq sponsored or was linked to 9/11, you could not stand the fact that Americans had that misapprehension — so you pounded us with the fact that there was no such link. (Along the way, you created the false impression that Bush had lied to them and said that there was a connection.)

If you had any principles, then surely right now, when the American people are set to blame President Bush and John McCain for a crisis they tried to prevent, and are actually shifting to approve of Barack Obama because of a crisis he helped cause, you would be laboring at least as hard to correct that false impression.

Your job, as journalists, is to tell the truth. That's what you claim you do, when you accept people's money to buy or subscribe to your paper.

But right now, you are consenting to or actively promoting a big fat lie — that the housing crisis should somehow be blamed on Bush, McCain, and the Republicans. You have trained the American people to blame everything bad — even bad weather — on Bush, and they are responding as you have taught them to.

If you had any personal honor, each reporter and editor would be insisting on telling the truth — even if it hurts the election chances of your favorite candidate.

Because that's what honorable people do. Honest people tell the truth even when they don't like the probable consequences. That's what honesty means. That's how trust is earned.

Barack Obama is just another politician, and not a very wise one. He has revealed his ignorance and naiveté time after time — and you have swept it under the rug, treated it as nothing.

Meanwhile, you have participated in the 'Borking' of Sarah Palin, reporting savage attacks on her for the pregnancy of her unmarried daughter — while you ignored the story of John Edwards's own adultery for many months.

So I ask you now: Do you have any standards at all? Do you even know what honesty means? Is getting people to vote for Barack Obama so important that you will throw away everything that journalism is supposed to stand for?

You might want to remember the way the National Organization of Women threw away their integrity by supporting Bill Clinton despite his well-known pattern of sexual exploitation of powerless women. Who listens to NOW anymore? We know they stand for nothing; they have no principles.

That's where you are right now.

It's not too late. You know that if the situation were reversed, and the truth would damage McCain and help Obama, you would be moving heaven and earth to get the true story out there.

If you want to redeem your honor, you will swallow hard and make a list of all the stories you would print if it were McCain who had been getting money from Fannie Mae, McCain whose campaign had consulted with its discredited former CEO, McCain, who had voted against tightening its lending practices.

Then you will print them, even though every one of those true stories will point the finger of blame at the reckless Democratic Party, which put our nation's prosperity at risk so they could feel good about helping the poor, and lay a fair share of the blame at Obama's door.

You will also tell the truth about John McCain: that he tried, as a Senator, to do what it took to prevent this crisis. You will tell the truth about President Bush: that his administration tried more than once to get Congress to regulate lending in a responsible way.

This was a Congress-caused crisis, beginning during the Clinton administration, with Democrats leading the way into the crisis and blocking every effort to get out of it in a timely fashion.

If you at our local daily newspaper continue to let Americans believe — and vote as if — President Bush and the Republicans caused the crisis, then you are joining in that lie.

If you do not tell the truth about the Democrats — including Barack Obama — and do so with the same energy you would use if the miscreants were Republicans — then you are not journalists by any standard. You're just the public relations machine of the Democratic Party, and it's time you were all fired and real journalists brought in, so that we can actually have a newspaper in our city.

Whoa! Thanks for your time, Jaq

Thursday, October 23, 2008

Are the presidential polls really accurate?

by J. Wright

National columnist Michael Barone wrote an interesting Internet article on presidential polls and their accuracy where he said in part, *"...this year especially, many who ask if we can trust the polls are usually concerned about something else: Can we trust the poll when one of the presidential candidates is black?*

"It is commonly said that the polls in the 1982 California and the 1989 Virginia gubernatorial races overstated the margin for the black Democrats who were running -- Tom Bradley and Douglas Wilder. The theory to account for this is that some poll respondents in each case were unwilling to say they were voting for the white Republican.

So, if I'm understanding Mr. Barone accurately, many white folks, when polled, may respond in favor of a black candidate, if there is one. In this case, that would be Senator Obama. Inside the voting booth, they may vote their conscience, perhaps NOT voting for Senator Obama. Afterward, if polled while exiting, they may state that they favored Obama, essentially skewing the pollster's results.

(Jaq's note: How disastrous would it be to eliminate poll taking altogether? In too many cases, the outcome is a result of how a question is posed.)

Going a step farther, *IF* Obama then loses to Senator McCain, all we'll hear from the left for months on end is, 'voter fraud; voter suppression; another stolen election!' Add to this, we may see litigation in many of the states where the vote difference was close; litigation in hopes of overturning the initial vote count in favor of the loser. We watched this agonizing spectacle in 2000 when vice-president Gore attempted to use the Florida State Supreme Court to "cherry pick" several select counties for a partial recount in order to circumvent George W. Bush's eventual small lead. Unfortunately, due to the months of <u>possibly inaccurate political polling statistics,</u>

what took place in Florida in 2000 may look like a walk-in-the-park in 2008.

For Michael Barone's complete article, go to:
http://online.wsj.com/article/SB122463210033356561.html?mod=dj emEditorialPage

Thanks for your time, Jaq

Sunday, October 26, 2008

Obama Campaign Cuts Off Interviews With Florida TV Station

Stolen from the Internet...

Biden gets asked tough questions by Orlando reporter
FOXNews.com Saturday, October 25, 2008 -

Barack Obama's campaign killed all interviews with a Florida TV station after Sen. Joe Biden, the Democratic vice presidential nominee, faced tough and critical questions from a reporter at the Orlando station, the Orlando Sentinel reported.

During a satellite video Thursday, WFTV's Barbara West quoted Karl Marx and asked Biden how Obama's comment to "Joe the Plumber," about spreading the wealth wasn't being Marxist.

"Are you joking?" Biden asked.

West replied, "No."

Later in the interview West questioned Biden about his comments that if Obama wins the election next month, he would be tested early on as president and wanted to know if Biden was implying America was no longer the world's leading power.

"I don't know who's writing your questions?" Biden asked her.

The Obama camp then killed a WFTV interview with Biden's wife Jill, according to an Orlando Sentinel blog.

"This cancellation is non-negotiable, and further opportunities for your station to interview with this campaign are unlikely, at best, for the duration of the remaining days until the election," wrote Laura K. McGinnis, Central Florida communications director for the Obama campaign, according to the Sentinel.

Such arrogance, and that's on top of the "Politics of Personal Destruction" the Obama-Biden camp along with their media friends used on an ordinary citizen, Samuel J. "Joe the plumber" Wurzelbacher, aka not to mention the ongoing scurrilous attacks almost daily on Republican vice-presidential candidate, Governor Sarah Palin.

The Obama folks seem intent in following old WWII Gestapo and Cold War KGB tactics; silence or attack the critics, AND they haven't taken office yet. The next several years should be interesting.

Thanks for your time, Jaq

Monday, October 27, 2008
More on Obama's Socialistic Cravings
by J. Wright

Earlier, a friend of mine applauded Socialism on our local newspaper's op-Ed page, listing our Social Security system, Medicare and the Post Office as fine examples. I agree to a point; believing that most anything, if administered in moderation, is acceptable. But for a presidential candidate to openly campaign on "spreading the wealth around," or in plain terms to take a portion of your hard earned money or savings and hand it over to someone else is nothing but socialism at its worst. At its best: it's thievery. To me, neither are acceptable.

Presidential candidate Obama told his Senate colleagues on March 7, 2007: "Let's stop sending mixed messages. Let's work together and set immigration fees at a level that are fair and consistent with our commitment to being an open, democratic, and egalitarian society."

Quoting Canadian journalist Marinka Peschmann, "Egalitarianism is defined as 'a social and political philosophy asserting the equality of all men, especially in their access to the rights and privileges of their society.' It's a social 'philosophy advocating the removal of inequalities among people.' The objective of egalitarianism advocacy is socialism.

"Socialism is 'a stage of society in Marxist theory transitional between capitalism and communism and distinguished by unequal distribution of goods and pay according to work done.' It's founded on two tenets: Thomas Jefferson's, 'All men are created equal,' in the Declaration of Independence and Karl Marx's 'From each according to his ability, to each according to his needs'."

History proves that socialists offer few practical points about how these two principles can be reconciled where everyone's quality of life is harmoniously lifted up instead of knocked down, (snip) capitalism may be the 'uneven distribution of wealth,' but 'socialism' is 'the even distribution of poverty.'

I pray we won't wake up one day and discover we've quietly become a socialistic welfare state, beginning with punishing of the successful. On the other hand, is it too late already?

Marinka Peschmann quotes a source:
http://canadafreepress.com/index.php/article/5839

Thanks for your time, Jaq

Tuesday, October 28, 2008

Why the Silence Concerning the Palin Effigy?

by J. Wright

Many times words left unspoken convey more meaning than an ear-splitting shout. That appears to be the case with the Obama Campaign's lack of response regarding the Sarah Palin effigy hanging by a noose from the gable of a West Hollywood CA residence. Quoting FOX NEWS.com, "The owner of a home that has a mannequin dressed like the Republican vice presidential candidate and hanging by a rope says, it's just a 'scary' Halloween decoration."

Yes, and right above it mounted atop a wide chimney is a likeness of Senator John McCain, Republican presidential hopeful, shrouded in flames. More Halloween fun I presume.

What concerns me is the utter silence emanating from the Obama camp, especially with the likeness of Governor Sarah Palin hanging by a rope. Politics being what it is today, what would the media's response be if a likeness of Democrat presidential candidate Barack Obama were seen hanging from a rope? OMG! I'm guessing there would be near riots in the streets accompanied by the hue and cry of racism along with a demand for John McCain to immediately repudiate the act. To date, no such outcry has been heard from the media demanding Obama repudiate the sexist Palin effigy. Is this the behavior we should expect during the next four years if Obama is elected president?

The national media have obviously been soft on the Obama Campaign from the beginning, so much so as to be labeled "in their pocket." Wonderful. When the honest media ruffles the feathers of the Obama camp, they are immediately chastised, placed in an unfavorable category and not allowed to contact or interview them further, as is the case in Orlando, Florida now where in an interview, a local TV station's reporter asked several uncomfortable questions of Joe Biden. Must we now condone selective free speech?

Following WW II and during the Cold War, the former USSR had its Tass and Pravda, their "official" news sources. What name will our biased media pick for themselves later in time?

Source: http://elections.foxnews.com/2008/10/27/effigy-palin-hanging-noose-halloween-fun-says-owner/)

Thanks for your time, Jaq

Saturday, November 1, 2008
Thomas Jefferson: Wealth Redistribution-
by J. Wright

Of late, there has been much said and discussed regarding "spreading the wealth around a little bit", which for the uninformed is simply allowing the government, or someone else, to take a portion of your income or savings and give it away. Don't confuse this with charity where one gives to the disadvantaged of their own volition, free will.

Thomas Jefferson, patriot, one of the nation's original Founders, best known as the author of the Declaration of Independence and third president of the United States, wrote in a letter to Joseph Milligan, April 6, 1816: *"To take from one, because it is thought his own industry and that of his fathers has acquired too much, in order to spare to others, who, or whose fathers, have not exercised equal industry and skill, is to violate arbitrarily the first principle of association, the guarantee to everyone the free exercise of his industry and the fruits acquired by it."*

For decades, this has been the foundation of our free enterprise system. One of the presidential candidates doesn't seem to accept that premise. If you agree with that premise, you'll know for whom to vote on Tuesday November 4.

Thanks for your time, Jaq

Monday, November 3, 2008

My 2-cents on the Election Outcome

by J. Wright

My 2-cents ... when all the dust has settled on election 2008, McCain-Palin will be the winners. That's _my_ opinion; and if I'm wrong, it won't be the first time.

As political analyst Dick Morris has said repeatedly, *IF* Senator Obama's poll numbers are at 49% or lower, *(giving Ralph Nader 1or 2%)* and Senator McCain can stay within 2-3% points, there are enough "undecided" out there to boost McCain past him. Then take into account those whom the pollsters called but didn't participate in the polls, the non-participants that I believe are mostly conservative. You know those 'bitter clingers who tend to take refuge in their church and their guns' and who have probably rolled the words "President Obama" around in their mouths and had it feel something akin to being third world.

I wouldn't be surprised to see a strong victory for the underdog, and with enough separation to not allow the Dems to cry "voter suppression!" Especially if we have a repeat of Gore-Lieberman 2000 with Obama receiving more popular votes *(based on massive black voter turnouts in the states that are Blue already)*, while McCain wins the Electoral College votes.

However it turns out, we'll finally be rid of the incessant political ads now running on our TV day and night. We have one dumpy little state representative here in northern lower-Michigan that is running the dumbest TV ad I've ever seen. His "thing" is that he can't be "bought" by the rich and powerful forces that are backing his opponent and he needs our help *(our vote I guess)* to "fight them."

Very intriguing. Very silly . . . in northern Michigan I can't imagine any "rich and powerful forces" that are interested in one small district mostly covered by forests with many dirt roads and a small village here and there. This is NOT the south side of Chicago by any means. Anyway, VOTE tomorrow, unless your have already.

Thanks for your time, Jaq

Wednesday, November 5, 2008

OK, it's over, I was wrong, now what?

by J. Wright

First: my "2-cents" worth of predicting an upset victory for Senator John McCain went down the toilet like many others dreams on Election night.

Second: sincere congratulations are in order to president-elect Barack Obama, I truly wish him luck.

A close friend from California, knowing that I was not voting for Barack Obama, emailed me Wednesday and asked, "How are you dealing with it?"

I replied that I had dealt with it on Election night while watching the TV screen and acknowledging that in my heart I knew McCain was really a loser, and with that, I turned off the TV and enjoyed a decent night's rest.

Two things came to mind in answering my friend: McCain may have picked a future winner with Alaska Governor Sarah Palin, regardless of whatever one will now hear from the McCain camp about her inexperience *(a lot of it possibly coming from some Romney-ites who worked for McCain after the primaries. Are they worried about 2012 already?)*

Second, John McCain really exonerated former Senator Robert Dole *(as I posted earlier)* in running the worst presidential campaign in Republican Party history. However, that's what the media expected; what they wanted, and in my opinion, this is the first time the media actually picked both candidates and controlled who the next president would be.

Now, I actually feel sorry for president-elect Obama. I still don't think he's experienced enough for the office and it will be sad watching him attempt to grow into it.

Picking ex-Clinton White House operative Rahm Emanuel as his Chief of Staff *(if he does)* would show me that Obama, may NOT be about "Change" at all. Emanuel is a rabid, hardheaded, North Chicago partisan who is not interested in "crossing the aisle" to serve the best interests of the country. He is more about the party. Emanuel said in a recent interview, "Republicans can go fuck themselves".

Unless Emanuel has suddenly changed his stripes, he intends to run the Republican Party out of business. That's hardly "reaching across the aisle." Is this the "Change That We Can Believe In? " I pray not.

Thanks for your time, Jaq

Friday, November 7, 2008

A Polite Re-hash...

by J. Wright

A long time Internet friend of mine, Mr. Alan Sherman, attorney at law and professional "world traveler extraordinaire" recently added my name to a political emailing list of his; a broad, informed list containing many of his friends and acquaintances from across the planet.

One of his friends in particular struck my fancy with his sensible postings and it's my pleasure to share part of a recent exchange we had prior to the election, or immediately afterward, one . . . allow me to introduce K. Murphy:

Re: George W. Bush

Jaq posted in part: What JFBurk *(another long time Internet friend)* posted earlier is similar to my opinion. GWB initially offered to bring a "new tone"" to Washington, DC and look what it got him; the most maligned president since Abraham Lincoln *(and look where Lincoln's place in American history is today)*.

K. Murphy's response: Actually, by the end of Lincoln's presidency he was greatly loved and respected. Warren Harding, Ulysses S. Grant *(who I greatly respect even though I am a southerner)*, Calvin Coolidge and Jimmy Carter were maligned at the end of their presidencies and history *(with the possible exception of Grant)* has not treated them well.

I truly hope that GWB winds up with a high place in our presidential list but I sorely doubt it. Bush did not really realize he was the President until 9/11. Attorney General John Ashcroft created a new category called a "person of interest." This is McCarthyism at its worst. No more is a person innocent until proven guilty. He *(Bush)* had *(Secretary of Defense)* Rummy, a man who did not listen to his generals and as a result did not put enough units into Iraq *(putting aside whether we should be there or not-- if we go in we should at least try to win.)* It took four years before we had a strategy that seems to be working. Bush abdicated his responsibilities and let the neocons take over. Shame on him.

From 9/11 on the Dems gave him everything he wanted. Look at the financial cost of the war and yet we do not have Bin Laden, even when we had the chances. I do not like Michael Moore but maybe there is truth to the comments about Bush's relationship with Bin Laden's family. Further, we are no safer in the world than before.

Finally, in 2006 the Dems started to have some backbone and said, "Enough is enough!" Can they be effective leaders? Only time will tell but I do not think they can do any worse than what we have had. It is convenient to blame the current financial crisis on Clinton and Greenspan-- they deserve a share of the blame no doubt, but Bush has been in charge of the nation and the economy since 2001.

I spent five years in the USMC and as an officer when I took command; everything related to that command was my responsibility even if the problem predated my command. Shouldn't it be the same for Bush? It does not seem so. He has been in charge of the economy for almost eight years. He had plenty of time to correct problems. *(By the way, Truman said the buck stopped here- He understood command, responsibility and accepted it.)* He (Bush) did not do it *(correct the problems)* and the financial crisis fell on his and McCain's head like a ton of bricks.

The fact is the Republican Party has been controlled by the neocons and the Christian Taliban. It is time that true conservatives take back their party and quit complaining about the Democrats, Clinton, and Obama. When they do, I will probably vote with them. While I like McCain as a person, he was not the right choice. He further aggravated the problem by choosing someone that made the Christian Taliban happy but not the rest of the country. About 56 million people felt it was time for a change. I agree with them.

Finally, one of the people in this email pointed out that the Prisoners at GitMo are not covered under the Geneva Convention. OK. Then they should be covered under America's laws. Further, no president in our past has ever authorized torture as acceptable national policy. Shame on him and the fact that he allowed such a policy to be acceptable. We stand for much more than that. Have a great day.

K. Murphy

Jaq responds: Well said, K. Murphy, I find little to agree with in much of what you wrote, but I don't chose to nit-pick. However, one could write pages on the obstacles the Dems placed in GWB's way during the first six years before they took over in 2006. Non-stop obstructionism IMO.

Post-Election, GWB got off to a bad start; at least that's my recollection. First, the "dangling chad" fiasco in Florida allowed VP Al Gore an attempt to cherry pick Dem strongholds for recounts that led to the SCOTUS telling the FSSC to go pack sand.

Bush definitely got off to a because of that hassle, IMO at least. It took him forever to get his administration approved and in place to the point of keeping some Clinton appointees; Tenet, for one. Questionable to say the least. At the same time, we had two Senate majority leaders, Trent Lott & Tom Daschle, who "shared" that post on and off for a while. Talk about gridlock.

In May of 2001, Vermont's Republican Senator Jim Jeffords decided to jump ship, switching parties allowing Daschle to run the Senate for the next 19 months. Adding to that mess, the country was coming out of a Clinton tenured recession brought about by the bursting of the tech bubble. Blue-collar friends of mine in the construction industry were losing big bucks fast from there 401s and weren't too happy about it. Of course, the media took the bait and began beating up Bush, claiming ad nauseum that the economy was "in the tank." It never stopped. All that prior to 9/11.

Barring another one of those national tragedies, president-elect Obama will have it better, although if Rahm Emanuel decides to be Chief of Staff, we might forget about "coming together."

He is more partisan than Karl Rove ever thought of being, even his friends say so.

I totally agree with your assessment of how the Iraq incursion could have been handled better. *(Especially in the later stages following the fall of Baghdad and Saddam's capture.)* Too many bureaucratic egos imbedded at the Department of State, Defense, CIA and in our military at first . . . *(Many left-overs from the previous Clinton Administration).*

We were basically at "war" with ourselves for several years. Sadly, we took Iraqi exile leader Ahmad Chalabi at his word at first, an Iraqi politician who hadn't been in country since 1958? Leader, or 'Community Organizer'? Geesh!

I am also of the opinion that the entire eight years of Bill Clinton's tenure were an unbelievable waste of a great talent *(and mistakes as well)*. Remember, he had his 'shot' at taking out Usama too. Too bad ol' Bill didn't govern as he could have.

My biggest disappointment during the last decade is how the national media have unashamedly and outwardly crawled into bed with the elitist, progressive liberals. Instead of reporting facts, as is their journalistic mission, they are seeming to emulate Woodard and Bernstein, or trying to be opinion columnists. Pretty infantile, IMO.

The same goes for the broadcast media, and we can thank CBS's confessed liberal, Walter Cronkite, in part for that. *(Remember Tet? Our military won that battle, yet Walter, in his steel helmet and looking knowledgeable on camera, said we lost. What we lost was CBS' credibility. Remember Dan Rather and his forged records of GWB's National Guard career?)* Where are the new Edward R. Morrows?

Regards, thanks for your time, Jaq

Thursday, November 13, 2008
<u>Obama and the Faltering Economy</u>
by J. Wright

I'm not an expert on the economy by any means, and by the looks of what's happening in the markets here and abroad today, it appears that nobody else fits that description either.

However, on November 1, three days before the presidential election, <u>Australian.news.com</u> quotes NEWS Corporation Chairman Rupert Murdoch in saying Barack Obama *'could worsen crisis.'*

Since the election, the market has lost 14% of its value. That on top of what it lost in the few weeks before the election when the $700-billion *(70% of a trillion, or about 26% of our 2008 federal budget of $2.6-trillion.)* bailout legislation passed by Congress.

Being retired and living on a fixed income shoestring, I'm not an investor, but if I were, I'd be converting any investment holdings to cash in a heartbeat.

Looking over the "new hires" that President-elect Obama has in the fold thus far, it appears to be "Clinton II", and we all should remember what was happening to the market at the end of Clinton's tenure; it wasn't pretty then. Why should it be different today or tomorrow with many of the same folks getting ready to run the show again?

With Obama's constant pushing for another "stimulus" package, when the first one didn't work, and his penchant for "saving" the Detroit auto industry' *(read: the UAW pensioners etal)* along with his seeming eagerness to spend tax money that doesn't exist, save for the printing presses, it's obvious to me why the market is skittish, saying the least. We saw it coming near the end of the campaign. As candidate Obama's stock *(polls)* began to rise, the market dropped. With the exception of a couple of recent spikes, it really hasn't stopped.

Quoting Murdoch again, *"To some extent it is beyond the power of politicians. You are going to find that the politicians are very limited in what they can do: they can make it worse but they can't stop it."*

Noted economist Lawrence Kudlow wrote recently:

In a few weeks Barack Obama will inherit the mantle of the capitalist system. What will he do with this responsibility? That's the question being asked everywhere.

Since the election, and up until President Bush's important G-20 speech, stock markets sold off nearly 15 percent. Investors want to know if economic rewards will be encouraged or penalized. Will trade remain open and free? Will we maintain competitive businesses that can compete worldwide? Or will we resort to the protection of ailing or failed businesses? Will the U.S. lurch toward the semi-socialism of Old Europe? Or will we stay with free-market capitalism? Will we expand the nanny-state economy? Or will we keep the door wide open to entrepreneurial spirit and gales of creative destruction?

Investors want to know which way President-elect Obama is going to go. Might he reach back to the Democratic pro-growth supply-side policies of John F. Kennedy's tax cuts, free trade, and strong dollar? Will he opt for Bill Clinton's free-trade and strong-dollar policies, or even his capital-gains tax cut? Or will he fall back to the hopeless government tinkering of Jimmy Carter or the welfare-statism of Lyndon Johnson?

I'm keeping an open mind on Mr. Obama during this post-election honeymoon period. After all, he stole the tax-cut issue from Sen. McCain during the election. Surely he knows the conservative red states that joined his campaign for change didn't vote for a leftward lurch to socialism lite.

Mr. Obama has a huge opportunity and an outsized responsibility to mend and revive the economy. It may be too much to ask, but perhaps he will give President Bush's marvelous speech a close read. There is much wisdom there. And there is no iron-clad reason why a Democrat can't adopt the economic-growth model that has worked so well and so long for this country.

— Larry Kudlow, NRO's Economics Editor, is host of CNBC's <u>Kudlow & Company</u> and author of the daily web blog, <u>Kudlow's Money Politic$</u>.

Thanks for your time, Jaq

Tuesday, November 18, 2008
<u>The Pending "Auto industry" Bailout</u>
by J. Wright

FYI, I'm a native of Michigan who retired on a fixed-income shoestring and I live "Up North" in Cadillac. Ten years ago, while living in Colorado, I vacationed in Michigan for a short time. One evening after shopping at the new Wal-Mart in Alma and walking back to my car, I noticed that EVERY automobile parked in the row with my Chevy rental car happened to be American made. Curious, I drove around the entire lot and didn't see a single foreign nameplate in the place. *'Remarkable,'* I thought to myself. *'My old Michigan friends and neighbors are really supporting our home-grown auto industry'.* Now it's 2008, what a difference 10 years makes, hmm?

In my lifetime, I have bought and owned *(even sold)* nothing but American made cars, the majority of them being Chrysler products. I wonder how many of the folks clamoring for an additional $25-billion for the Detroit auto industry can say the same thing?

A report last week said the average American-made auto hourly costs are more than $70.00, compared with the average foreign nameplate, even those built down south, are around $40.00. Quite a difference.

Union vs. non-union? Corporate management?

Several years ago, maybe three, I read on line where a UAW member mowing grass at a Saginaw MI factory was earning more than $70.00 hourly including his benefits. He must have been one highly talented individual to deserve that kind of money.

I spent most of a lifetime working in construction. With my God-given talent, I can build a house, or most anything else from the ground up with the help of a few semi-skilled grunts for muscle. During my career as an hourly worker, I never earned more than $33.50 per hour, with no benefits. Qualified as 'Skilled' when I worked in the trades, I had to invest more than $8,000 in tools in order to earn that much. Maybe I should'a invested in a good lawnmower instead.

I'm not complaining, it was my choice, just as it was the automakers choice to cave in to organized labor and be tied up in massive labor and benefit contracts that now have come home to roost.

The taxpayers previously made a $25 billion "loan" to the auto industry for future retooling in hopes of manufacturing a "green" automobile one-day, now we are asked to do it again. My question is simple: where does that kind of money come from? Printing presses? And how much of it will be going to bail out the UAW? And the pensioners that are NOT working but are ENTITLED to fat retirement checks and health benefits according to their previous contracts with the automakers?

As you may know, when Uncle Sam (federal government) gets involved in anything, many times the situation deteriorates and becomes worse. I don't want, and we don't need, Senator Harry Reid and House Speaker Nancy Pelosi, or even president-elect Barack Obama micro-managing the designing and manufacturing of our cars.

I say let the Detroit auto industry do what most any of us that don't qualify for massive government loans would be forced to do: file for bankruptcy, restructure, and start anew. Learn to operate their company's in a logical, mature, business-like manner for a change.

They could look at the successful American auto industry in the southern states and maybe follow their lead? Will it ever happen?

The Liberal Democrat politicians choose to use the expression "auto industry" when speaking of Detroit's "Big 3," including our next president, Mr. Obama. It's intentionally misleading. The Ford Motor Company refused bail-out funds, plus the American auto industry, outside of Detroit and Michigan in particular, is thriving; building new autos with foreign nameplates while using high quality American labor *(non-union of course.)*

The Ford Motor Company and the others are a major part of the "auto industry" and don't need, or want a bailout. Is Barack Obama's incessant "misspeak" a harbinger of things to come?

This latest $25 billion fiasco that Obama, Majority Leader Reid, and House Speaker Pelosi & Company want stuffed down the taxpayers' throats is nothing but a UAW labor union bailout, and guess what? The AP recently reported that UAW president Ron Gettlefinger says workers will not make any more concessions, and that getting the automakers back on their feet means figuring out a way to turn the economy around. *(No kidding. What an amazing grasp of the obvious.)* So, in essence, screw the taxpayers and the country; we got ours and we ain't gonna' budge.

Having lived in Michigan most of my life, it's my opinion that that type of attitude is what put us, and the auto industry, in the shape it's in today.

Just for the hell of it, did you know that GM has more non-working retired former employees receiving benefits and healthcare coverage today than it has actual auto builders in the factories? And GM will run out of money soon and won't be able to keep their promises agreed to in the 2007 contract agreements with the UAW. Talk about corporate mismanagement coupled with labor greed.

On top of that, with all of the multiple billions of dollars the elected representatives in D.C. are doling out today, this country is in hock more than $36 TRILLION in 'future unfunded mandates?' *(Future Social Security, Medicare/Medicaid promises/commitments made to our retirees and financially disadvantaged.)* Or is that $36 Trillion stored away in some secret "lock box?"

I think $36 TRILLION is more than the United States is worth if every bit of our combined assets, private and federal, were liquidated, and yet the politicians still get starry-eyed with their power to incessantly spend the taxpayers money. It has to end one day. Will it?

Thanks for your time, Jaq

Tuesday, December 16, 2008
The Needs of Special Interests Come Before Adhering to our Constitution
by J. Wright

An article in Saturday's Cadillac News, front page above the fold, stated: "Many in Michigan upset about bailout collapse." The article quoted UAW president Ron Gettlefinger and Michigan Governor Jennifer Granholm. Both had nasty words to say about U.S. Senate Republicans in particular. Several local residents added responsible remarks to the commentary; some in favor, some not.

Me? I'd merely suggest that our lawmakers, especially the U.S. House and Senate Democrats, who are heavily influenced by a major "special interest," namely the UAW that represents most auto-workers in our region, reread the 14th amendment of our U.S. Constitution; the part guaranteeing equal protection for all.

I'm not a constitutional scholar by any means. Many smarter people than me have responded to these bailouts, especially retired Judge Andrew Napolitano, as follows: *"Bailouts violate the Equal Protection doctrine because the Congress can't fairly pick and choose who to bail out and who to let expire. They violate the General Welfare Clause because they benefit only a small group and*

---

not the general public. They violate the Due Process Clause because they interfere with contracts already entered into, and they turn the public treasury into a public trough. Worse still, Congress lacks the power to let someone else decide how to spend the peoples' money. In effect, the Congress delegated to the Secretary of the Treasury some of the power the Constitution has delegated to the Congress: The power to decide when, how, for whose benefit, and in what amounts taxpayer dollars should be spent."

The key wording to me is that <u>Congress lacks the power to delegate someone else to spend the public's money</u>. They seem to forget that it's NOT the government's money; it's ours!

In effect, they are shredding the law of the land; our Constitution. I find that deplorable.

Thanks for your time, Jaq

2009

Thursday, January 15, 2009
America's Soft Underbelly?
by J. Wright

It's been a day short of a month since I penned something for this blog. My apologies, life happens...

I assisted Susan in driving her Toyota from northern Michigan to sunny Phoenix Arizona for her Dad, Albert, to buy. On our second day out we visited with my oldest daughter and her family in the Denver Colorado area. On the next day we trekked south for lunch in Santa Fe and spent the night in Gallup, New Mexico. Lots of open, uninhabited land out there and along the way. Leaving Gallup we drove to Flagstaff and spent an overnight with Susan's son and his family before driving south out of the snow to Phoenix. There I caught a nasty respiratory virus and am still ridding myself of that.

A lot has transpired since my last post. Some of it highly questionable.

One of president-elect Obama's choices for high office with a tremendous responsibility is the new pick to head our CIA *(Central Intelligence Agency),* Leon Paneta.

Leon is a friendly appearing sort, everyone's friend, but what the hell does he know about Intelligence? Time will tell I guess, it always does.

With that in mind, the following article is taken from an email that I received late today. Rather scary reading in my opinion. After reading it, maybe you'll agree that it's scary too.

Here goes: *"Juval Aviv was the Israeli Agent upon which the movie <u>Munich</u> was based. He was Golda Meir's bodyguard -- she appointed him to track down and bring to justice the Palestinian terrorists who took the Israeli athletes hostage and killed them during the Munich Olympic Games.*

In a lecture in New York City a few weeks ago, he shared information that EVERY American needs to know -- but that our government has not yet shared with us. He predicted the London subway bombing on the Bill O'Reilly show on Fox News stating publicly that it would happen within a week. At the time, O'Reilly laughed and mocked him saying that in a week he wanted him back on the show. But, unfortunately, within a week the terrorist attack had occurred.

Juval Aviv gave intelligence (via what he had gathered in Israel and the Middle East) to the Bush Administration about 9/11 a month before it occurred. His report specifically said they would use planes as bombs and target high profile buildings and monuments. Congress has since hired him as a security consultant.

Now for his future predictions. He predicts the next terrorist attack on the U.S. will occur within the next few months. Forget hijacking airplanes, because he says terrorists will NEVER try and hijack a plane again as they know the people onboard will never go down quietly again. Aviv believes our airport security is a joke -- that we have been reactionary rather than proactive in developing strategies that are truly effective.

For example: 1) Our airport technology is outdated. We look for metal, and the new explosives are made of plastic. 2) He talked about how some idiot tried to light his shoe on fire. Because of that, now everyone has to take off their shoes. A group of idiots tried to bring aboard liquid explosives. Now we can't bring liquids on board. He says he's waiting for some suicidal maniac to pour liquid explosive on his underwear; at which point, security will have us all traveling naked! Every strategy we have is 'reactionary.' 3) We only focus on security when people are heading to the gates.

Aviv says that if a terrorist attack targets airports in the future, they will target busy times on the front end of the airport when/where people are checking in. It would be easy for someone to take two suitcases of explosives, walk up to a busy check-in line, ask a person next to them to watch their bags for a minute while they run to the restroom or get a drink, and then detonate the bags BEFORE security even gets involved. In Israel, security checks bags BEFORE people can even ENTER the airport.

Aviv says the next terrorist attack here in America is imminent and will involve suicide bombers and non-suicide bombers in places where large groups of people congregate. (i. e., Disneyland, Las Vegas casinos, big cities (New York, San Francisco, Chicago, etc.) and that it will also include shopping malls, subways in rush hour, train stations, etc., as well as rural America this time (Wyoming, Montana, etc.).

The attack will be characterized by simultaneous detonations around the country (terrorists like big impact), involving at least 5-8 cities, including rural areas. Aviv says terrorists won't need to use suicide bombers in many of the larger cities, because at places like the MGM Grand in Las Vegas, they can simply valet park a car loaded with explosives and walk away.

Aviv says all of the above is well known in intelligence circles, but that our U. S. government does not want to 'alarm American citizens' with the facts. The world is quickly going to become 'a different place', and issues like 'global warming' and political correctness will become totally irrelevant.

On an encouraging note, he says that Americans don't have to be concerned about being nuked. Aviv says the terrorists who want to destroy America will not use sophisticated weapons. They like to use suicide as a front-line approach. It's cheap, it's easy, it's effective; and they have an infinite abundance of young militants more than willing to 'meet their destiny'.

He also says the next level of terrorists, over which America should be most concerned, will not be coming from abroad. But will be, instead, 'homegrown' -- having attended and been educated in our own schools and universities right here in the U. S. He says to look for 'students' who frequently travel back and forth to the Middle East. These young terrorists will be most dangerous because they will know our language and will fully understand the habits of Americans; but that we Americans won't know/understand a thing about them.

Aviv says that, as a people, Americans are unaware and uneducated about the terroristic threats we will inevitably face. America still has only have a handful of Arabic and Farsi speaking people in our intelligence networks, and Aviv says it is critical that we change that fact SOON. So, what can America do to protect itself?

From an intelligence perspective, Aviv says the U.S. needs to stop relying on satellites and technology for intelligence. We need to, instead, follow Israel's, Ireland's and England's hands-on examples of human intelligence, both from an infiltration perspective as well as to trust 'aware' citizens to help. We need to engage and educate ourselves as citizens; however, our U. S. government continues to treat us, its citizens, 'like babies.' Our government thinks we 'can't handle the truth' and are concerned that we'll panic if we understand the realities of terrorism. Aviv says this is a deadly mistake.

Aviv recently created/executed a security test for our Congress, by placing an empty briefcase in five well-traveled spots in five major cities. The results? Not one person called 911 or sought a policeman to check it out. In fact, in Chicago, someone tried to steal the briefcase!

In comparison, Aviv says that citizens of Israel are so well 'trained' that an unattended bag or package would be reported in seconds by citizen(s) who know to publicly shout, 'Unattended Bag!' The area would be quickly & calmly cleared by the citizens themselves. But, unfortunately, America hasn't been yet 'hurt enough' by terrorism for their government to fully understand the need to educate its citizens or for the government to understand that it's their citizens who are, inevitably, the best first-line of defense against terrorism.

Aviv also was concerned about the high number of children here in America who were in preschool and kindergarten after 9/11, who were 'lost' without parents being able to pick them up, and about ours schools that had no plan in place to best care for the students until parents could get there. (In New York City, this was days, in some cases!)

He stresses the importance of having a plan, that's agreed upon within your family, to respond to in the event of a terroristic emergency. He urges parents to contact their children's schools and demand that the schools, too, develop plans of actions, as they do in Israel.

Does your family know what to do if you can't contact one another by phone? Where would you gather in an emergency? He says we should all have a plan that is easy enough for even our youngest children to remember and follow.

Aviv says that the U. S. government has in force a plan that, in the event of another terrorist attack, will immediately cut-off EVERYONE's ability to use cell phones, blackberries, etc., as this is the preferred communication source used by terrorists and is often the way that their bombs are detonated.

How will you communicate with your loved ones in the event you cannot speak to them? You need to have a plan.

So there it is, boys and girls . . . one man's idea of what our future may hold. Pray he is mistaken.

Thanks for your time, Jaq~

Wednesday, January 21, 2009

"Soft Underbelly" article Follow-up

by J. Wright

I have had the rare pleasure *(at times)* of connecting with an online political discussion group for several years starting in the mid-1990s. One of the participants, known to me simply as <u>Sara,</u> is an Israeli female who splits time between Florida and Israel. She is over there now, but keeps in constant touch via her email communications.

In my previous article, I suggested that she might have some pertinent comments. She certainly did, and I have posted them here with her permission.

~ ~ ~

John,

Yes, I have a few comments ... (laughing) but of course you had to know that. What he's saying shouldn't come as a surprise to anyone on the list ... and Israeli's are not uniquely qualified to anticipate when and where terror will erupt. It just comes, it's an evolutionary process whereby the "don't haves," for whatever reason that they don't have, decide to make their presence and whatever point they feel they have known to the perceived "haves." (One can substitute meanies, imperialists, genocidal maniacs, modern-day Nazis, far-right fascists, or whatever euphemism one wants to for the "haves" in this case, as we have seen done over and over again).

I look at the situation as a "class struggle." <u>Ladyhkr</u> (another female email poster) looks at it as a "status struggle." <u>Fundy</u> (another female email poster) apparently looks at it as an "interrelated Muslim - over-populating (in comparison to the aborting euro-Caucasian-Christian populace) socio -economic discontented with their lot in life conspiracy to overtake the world that can only be brought to a halt under the leadership of Ron Paul's struggle that will, by the by, bankrupt us along the way, if it hasn't already.

Whatever it is, there is no question that the "powers that be" will continue to wage conventional wars and the "powers that aren't" will continue to attack the "soft underbelly".

Russian made BM-21 Grad rockets hit Beer Sheva yesterday, and I drove past it today thinking about the difference of when I was a kid here.

When I was a kid I'd hop on a bus and if there was an unattended package, you immediately reacted, like in the article. But more than that, before you sat down (anyplace, not just on a bus) you used your hand to "sweep the seat" to make sure that nothing was there that you might sit on/or over, because they used to leave bombs that would detonate upon physical pressure.

In America, people think nothing of sitting down on a public seat in an airport or someplace and putting their things on the seat next to them. In Israel you never did that. You would pile the things up underneath you, between your legs, on your lap, etc. But if something was on the seat, or beneath it, it was suspicious and you didn't so much as raise the alarm automatically, but you "swept the seat" by instinct just in case, and if something was there, people weren't blind to it but they reacted appropriately.

Those were the days before suicide bombers ... generations have now been born that don't even remember those types of threat, nowadays, you have to "sweep the surroundings," you literally have to eyeball everyone around, PROFILE, if you will ...and yes ...you are looking for people that look suspicious: Nervous, sweating, overdressed, not making eye contact, talking to themselves, or conversely in the zone of euphoria, as if they are already on their way to heaven, (which I think I'd find even more alarming).

I have faith in America. Americans are a remarkably resilient country, with a "can-do / kick-ass" attitude. We've shown it in the past. We are a nation of un-pedigreed mutts: and I say that with the greatest of respect.

Americans came to this country seeking a better life from the countries that they left, and at their core, beneath the soft, bloated, underbelly that we have developed from living a particularly easy life in comparison to most of the rest of the world. We have maintained a very healthy work ethic, a belief in a strong defense, a "Don't tread on me" mentality, an appreciation and sympathy for the underdog, all while still being a world leader in technological progress and economy.

We have balance in this country ... it enables us to roll with the punches and still come out swinging when the time comes.

We have had to change some of our travel habits a bit. We have had some of our liberties (from most of which we haven't felt any real interruptions to our lives) curtailed.

Some of our tax dollars have been siphoned off to pay for new "security systems." Big Deal. I really haven't felt any appreciable difference in my way of living in the USA, other than I am always sure to wear socks when flying commercial because I don't want to walk barefoot where millions of others do.

I have always felt that it was only a matter of time before terrorism (as opposed to pervasive violent crime) became a real problem in this country. And I think that it is probably well on its way here.

We've had salvos and shots across the bow. We've had Oklahoma City and 9-11. Direct hits, and I don't doubt that we will have more. I also don't doubt that we will be able to adjust and adapt to the attacks.

But PROFILING will have to become a part of our strategy against this. And in this case, the ACLU be damned. Pertinent questions will have to be addressed and the world of political correctness might have to be sacrificed on occasion when the question of the "greater good" is at hand.

Laws CAN and SHOULD be enacted so that the abuse of this does not occur, for instance, if crimes are detected un-related to national security, by routine national security profiling, they might not be acted upon. I'm not a legal mind to determine the ins and outs of this, BUT, it seems to me that there has to be more security involved, and that those that will cry "abuse of power" can relax a bit if there are some legal adjustments.

As for the issue of attacking where the crowds are, well, I think that's a given. it's sort of ingrained in me at this point to try and avoid huge crowds to optimize my comfort zone, and yet, there are times when I say, "To hell with it, fate is fate, and I'm going to enjoy myself and GO," but I do know that it is safer to get past the checkpoints in place when in airports, cruise embarkations, etc.

Just a few years ago, some whacko in LA attacked the exterior check-in area at the LAX airport near the EL AL counter, because they know they can't get past. The same has happened in Frankfurt Germany and Rome Italy.

I'm sure I could go on, but I actually have to go out now; bringing some dinner to the hospital here for Shabbat.

Shalom all, Sara

~ ~ ~

Thanks for your time, Jaq

Friday, January 23, 2009

A conversation: The Black Community's New Expectations

by J. Wright

Following the Inauguration, some of us in the political discussion group I mentioned earlier were discussing how President Obama might become a role model for the black inner city youngsters and maybe even their parents. The following is an email exchange between several of us.

··· ··· ···

Jim: I just heard another one of those Obama supporters who expects to be rich due to the fact that Obama is President! She stated, *"We ain't rich like you folks but will be one day because we have Barack Obama as President."*

Now isn't that special? Do you believe how dumb and naïve some people are? Can you imagine how suicidal this person is going to be when Obama fails to deliver on that expectation? What is wrong with people today with that cult mentality and their expectations for a handout that will make them rich? Was this country built on that mentality?

Alan: Absolutely not. In fact, I think it will get worse. I believe that many out there will have the attitude that they will be given a free pass because "one of theirs is in charge."

I believe that they will test the system more, expect more and, when they don't get it, will revolt.

Jaq: Well, they certainly have former Secretary of Labor *(under Clinton)* Robert Reich on their side. He's all for taking a portion of the "Stimulus infrastructure dollars" and handing it out to anyone except white male, skilled construction workers, contractors, etc. (per *Michelle Malkin » Robert Reich: Keep stimulus money away from skilled workers and "white male contractors."*)

There, boys and girls, is the beginning of a broadening welfare program to redistribute our future tax dollars *(and those of our kids and their kids as far as the eye can see.)* How much infrastructure will be improved while handing out billions to the disadvantaged? Of the nearly trillion dollar "Economic Stimulus Package," only about 4% was designated to infrastructure. Pitiful.

At some point, more than 50% of the damn population will either be federal employees or *po'* folks on the federal dole of some description. Then we'll be well on our way to a one party system. Democrats forever! Mercy ... the thought of it is revolting.

Alan: Hopefully I will be living nearly full time in Thailand by the time things get that bad. My kids are the ones that I worry about. My son will no doubt head back to Asia as soon as he graduates. Either Japan or China. My oldest daughter is pretty much settled with a very good job as a senior project director for a major construction company.

My youngest daughter is in her second year of Architecture and Design and has no problems moving back to Japan for her graduate degree in Architecture as she has an affinity towards Asian design.

Things don't look so good for the social structure of America. Once they removed God from our public lives, the rest went downhill fast. Liberalism is a disease whose only cure is getting what they actually want. Then it is too late. Therefore, liberalism is a terminal rotting, disease killing everything it touches.

Jaq: Alan, you are fortunate to be in such a position. What percent of the country could be as fortunate, .0001%? That leaves a lot of us, particularly the ones who DIDN'T vote for Obama, Pelosi, Reid & Company, holding the bag.

Myself, I may be close to being as fortunate as you considering my tender age... :) hell, I may die before the liberal/socialist bullshit becomes too deep. Even Hell might begin to look good as opposed to what this nation could become. Good luck, my friend.

Alan: I truly am blessed, Jack. In the great scheme of things, we all are. It was only the good fortune of being born in American while each of us had a chance that put is in the position we are today. Each of us here on this thread have worked hard all of our loves and made no excuses for the failures we have had along the way or the misfortunes that have been subject to. We took the good with the bad and just kept on going knowing that our generation will succeed and that our children's generation will do even better than we did.

We grew up in an America with a God, with a balanced political scene, with the American dream a reality for all. We saw Europe become socialized and watched it decay into a mere shadow of what it used to be. We looked at America and believed that we would never, never fall into that despair that fell on Europe. At least we felt that way until Vietnam began dividing our nation.

The leftist surge was sponsored by the communists and was all too eagerly signed on by the media with the likes of Walter Cronkite and other print and broadcast media 'all-stars'. They began with Nixon, forcing his resignation; a first. This gave them momentum and power. They next brought in an idiot of a peanut farmer who set the standards of a weak, meek and pacifist America.

As the young left-wingers grew up, they became the destructive force behind emasculating and changing America. They became and are the media, the Hollywood elite, the jetsam and flotsam of the hippy leftist generation whose first task was to eliminate God from our public lives. They are the liberal elitists who are nothing more than mini Czarists themselves.

They set forth an agenda of weakening America, setting one segment of the population against the other, turning right into wrong, removing censorship, promoting free and open sex and considering perverted relationships as normal.

How far has this country gone in so few years? Most of the nation still prefers a Ronald Reagan to a Barack Obama, but the powerful left has fully and totally undermined our nation by belittling our presidents, reducing the standards of education, scandalizing our sacred institutions of marriage and religion, minimizing the reality of the threats against us by our enemies, and kneeling before those that want to destroy us by bringing our social structure to its knees.

They have produced a 'divide and conquer' mentality amongst Americans by inciting class warfare, pushing gay agendas, caring more for the environment than for the humans who inhabit it, making us dependent upon foreign resources as well as foreign workers, allowing unions to dictate their own terms of employment thereby shutting down American businesses and weakening our positions in the world. I am fed up with these ingrates. These hypocritical ass-wipes who have no concept of the consequences of their actions. They don't deserve America but are more than willing to enjoy its rewards.

Lynn: Good grief, Alan, you sound almost like one of those 'gun clinging, right wing, Bible thumping fundamentalists.' **:)** I've asked a lot of people what do they think has caused our country's downward slide into being a few steps from a Sodom or Gomorrah. Most all start off with the removal of God from public life and national consciousness.

Of course, I think the same but then I'm one of those 'gun clinging, right wing, Bible thumping fundamentalists. It appears to me that when there is an acknowledgment and respect in something greater than yourself, be it God as I know Him, or a simple acknowledgment of a Higher Power that respect flows over into one's daily life.

By no means do I think a believing people are near perfect, but the majority of people seem to have an internal guidance system to be a little more honest, a little more courteous, a little more respectful of others, and more responsible.

There is a hope, enthusiasm, and an expectation for tomorrow. I'm not deluded that we'd have a Utopia, or had a Utopia, but this country is consumed by greed, and reeks of dishonesty. An air of gloom and victimhood permeates the atmosphere.

Our political leaders look out for themselves and are consumed with securing more money, more prestige, more power, and insuring their reelection. There is no love or loyalty for this country, only what they personally can obtain. I am thankful that I lived at our zenith and deeply sadden and distressed as it slowly dissolves.

Alan: You are spot on, Lynn. It has nothing to do with religion or being a religious zealot. It has to do with the acknowledgment that there is someone greater than us. Someone upon whom the Founding Fathers based the birth of our nation.

If we look at the alternative, we wind up with Soviet dominated communism. We also see the void that China went through during the Maoist revolutions. Remove God from the people and they only have the government to look up to as their Godhead.

The liberals in this country are doing just that. Even Russian and China knew, as witnessed by freedom of religion in China now and same in Russia and the old Soviet states, that you can't control the people for long. Something the liberals will never get.

Liberalism has not learned nor is willing to learn. You can't strip God from our lives, remove him from schools, and remove him from courthouses and government establishment. It appears to be the bond that allows us the greatness and the freedom needed for the wellbeing of our nation.

Liberals substituted humanism. They cloak their agenda under the banner of PC. The desire not to ever hurt someone's feelings, even if it decays the inner fabric of America and undermines the will of the vast majority of Americans. Heading up this liberal cause is the ACLU, better known as the new American Communist Party.

It is a sad day when the people of America are too timid to take back from this left wing minority what is theirs. Their rights to express their beliefs in schools, government oaths, civic auditoriums and public functions.

Jim: I couldn't agree with you more, great post. You and I have many similarities and I really relate to your post. I have said on this thread how happy I am with my life. I have a wonderful family and we are close so I must have done something right growing up.

I cannot help but notice how unhappy many liberals are and it seems they want to spread their misery equally to everyone else. I will never forget growing up in a relatively poor family and being taught that I could do anything that I wanted to do but that there are consequences for choices made. Over the years I made many mistakes but never booted God out of my life or my family's life.

I started out as a Democrat and the first President I supported was JFK however wasn't old enough to vote at the time. I remember the Communist years and how we were told that Communism will bury us. At the time I thought that meant militarily but grew to learn that they would destroy us from within and without a shot being fired. I see that happening today as God is being removed from our lives and there is a moral decay today sweeping this country led by the secular progressives whose live for today ideology ignores personal responsibility. I have yet to hear any liberal blame themselves for personal problems they created.

I believed strongly in the American dream and knew that I could achieve that dream with hard work, dedication, and the right mental attitude. I never relied on any President to take care of me and to make my life better although I knew that a President could hurt us by raising taxes and by failure to keep us safe. Those therefore remained the two most important issues for me in any election.

Today I see the hero worship, cult mentality of so many. "Save me, Mr. President, from mistakes I have made", "I will never have to pay my mortgage or for gasoline again" seem to be the cry of far too many. The swooning, fainting, stars in the eyes, and unrealistic expectations of one individual simply doesn't' make any sense to me. This attitude wasn't prevalent when I was growing up so what happened to us?

Could it be the removal of God from so many lives? I believe that is part of the problem along with the instant gratification crowd that lives for today instead of planning for tomorrow. In today's world everyone lets the things they want get in the way of actually getting the things they need. This entitlement mentality where everyone deserves a home, everyone deserves healthcare, everyone deserves a living wage ignores the fact that all these are EARNED not guaranteed. The economic and historic ignorance of so many is staggering. I see it all the time on this thread, but more importantly in real reported in the media.

I will continue to keep things in the proper perspective and focus on that which I can control. I will remain proactive instead of being reactive and will never lose my positive attitude and will refuse to participate in the liberal negative rhetoric and creation of victims. That is why I always appreciate your posts.

Jocelyn: What's scary is her scenario could come true. That ($350-billion) stimulus package that Obama is putting forward is earmarked especially for those people. You heard what Robert Reich had to say, didn't you? Granted, he's just an advisor but lets be clear, he is an advisor for a reason.

When he says that the Administration has to find a way to cut out skilled individuals and that includes construction workers and focus on the chronically unemployed or unemployable to receive stimulus cash *($350-billion)* in rebuilding our infrastructure, that should be taken to mean something like a promise. The Administration will pave that way forward. Obama campaigned on redistribution of wealth and anyone who thinks he's suddenly going to become a centrist is fooling themselves. These people aren't as dumb as we are for thinking that her scenario of becoming "rich" by her standards because her President is in office won't happen.

This President must not succeed. Now it's we who have to find a way to make that happen because our *(Republican)* leadership such as it is, is too busy holding their ankles.

••• ••• •••

Thanks for your time, Jaq

Friday, January 30, 2009

"Change You Can Believe In?" Wrong!

by J. Wright

(This opinion piece of mine was published January 29, in the Cadillac, MI, News.)

"Change You Can Believe In?" You must be joking. $850 billion taxpayer dollars spread over a 647 page bill, HR-1, the "American Recovery and Reinvestment Act" is being rushed through the House of Representatives. It's referred to as a "Stimulus and Job Creation Package." Your taxpayer dollars are supposed to stimulate our economy and shorten the recession, but will take years to take effect, won't create many actual jobs. Call it what it is; "Porkification." Here's part of what the Congressional Democrat lawmakers propose:

1. $4.19 billion to ACORN – (OMG!) A questionable, far left political organization.

2. $200 million for the beautification of the National Mall, including $21 million for sod. *(Note: this was removed via a Republican amendment before the House vote, as was one other minor spending item.)*

3. Over $200 million for contraceptives and the abortion industry.

4. $650 million for digital TV coupons.

5. $136 billion to create at least 32 new government programs – more than a third of H.R.1's spending provisions would go towards growing the government — not the economy.

6. $600 million for new cars for the federal bureaucrats.

7. $50 million for the National Endowment of the Arts. *(This may have been the other spending item removed.)*

8. $6 billion for colleges and universities –many of whom already have billion dollar endowments.

9. $300 billion to bail out *selected* state governments – "Wealth redistribution?" Are the days over of state governments taking care of themselves and balancing their own budgets? *(Of that $300-billion, $140 billion goes to additional education funding, doing absolutely nothing to stimulate the economy or create jobs.)*

10. Increased spending on more than 150 existing federal programs. *(The Wall Street Journal published an article saying that less than 5%, or only $5-billion of this massive boon-doggle would be spent on job creating infrastructure such as bridge and highway repair, which I previously mentioned; the actual amount was about 4.1%).*

In summary, this list illustrates that Congressional Democrats have little intention of actually stimulating the economy, and the "American Recovery and Reinvestment Act" comes up embarrassingly short on efforts to cut taxes in any meaningful way. The nation is facing near bankruptcy and it appears the liberals are attempting to spend our way into prosperity.

Additionally, when this HR-1 passed the House, with 'Yea' votes consisting of just Democrats, and with all 177 Republicans and 11 Democrats in opposition, the Senate then added more spending raising the total to about $900 billion (90% of a trillion). Add in the eventual interest this bill will cost, because there is NO money in the national treasury to fund it, the costs will exceed more than $1 trillion, according to the Congressional Budget Office. Isn't that precious? Congress just indebted every family in the country another $6,700.00.

Republican Senate Minority Leader Mitch McConnell said in effect, "This isn't a stimulus bill, it's a spending bill."

If it looks like a pig and walks like a pig, it's probably a pig, and that's PORK friends. There's still time to call your particular United States Senator and hope that your thoughts will be heard.

Thanks for your time, Jaq

Tuesday, February 3, 2009

<u>Change? Same ol' Deceitful Crap;</u>
<u>Different Faces.</u>

by J. Wright

It's interesting how many times during the past eight years that we heard the words, "Bush lied!" When the dust settled and we examined his words, they weren't exactly lies at all, but more like wishful thinking by those engaged in what later became known as "Bush Derangement Syndrome." That was then.

Now we have a shiny new administration in Washington, one whose major premise whilst campaigning was that "Fundamental Change" was on the horizon; a new era of political ethics and transparency was coming our way. Huh?

First, former New Mexico Governor Bill Richardson withdrew his name for Commerce Secretary because of some shady "pay-for-play" dealings that are still under investigation. Then we are presented with Eric Holder, a questionable nominee for Attorney General, who, had he been a Republican would have been sent packing. Instead he was confirmed by the Democrats in the Senate.

Following that, Timothy Geithner, who previously failed to pay the IRS all its due ($25,970.00) now heads up the Treasury Department which also oversees the IRS. Hey! The guy is sharp, and in our current state of national economic crisis; the "best" man for the job!

This was followed by former Democrat Senate Majority Leader Tom Daschle, who didn't pay more than $140,000 in taxes or even bother to report it; he'll possibly be our next HUD Secretary. His excuse? "I forgot." Good grief, could you or I get away with a simple "I forgot?" Yet, Obama's pick for Performance post, Czarina Nancy Killefer, withdrew her name over a potential income tax problem. *(Within hours after I wrote this post, Tom Daschle withdrew his name from contention.)* Bully!

"Is this really the message he *(Obama)* wants to convey *(snip),* a message that it's O.K. to break or skirt the law just as long as you're a good guy with a special skill?" asked Andy Ostroy, a blogger writing on the liberal Huffington Web site.

During the campaign, Candidate Obama said he would <u>not allow</u> former lobbyists in his administration: already he has named at least three, possibly a fourth. His excuse: *there are hundreds of posts to be filled and hiring three that are previous lobbyists is not a problem.* It is to me President Obama, *IF* you say you aren't going to hire the first one and then proceed to break your word. *(Lie?)*

Worse, Candidate Obama pledged to ban earmarks from future Congressional bills *(AKA "bringin' home the bacon!")* yet he doesn't seem concerned with this massive taxpayer funded "$817 billion *(non)*-Stimulus" bill being considered in the Senate. *(Reportedly, it's getting bigger . . . worse in other words,)*

Change? Same ol' deceitful crap; different faces. That's the way it appears from my living room.

Thanks for your time, Jaq

Friday, February 6, 2009
<u>More "old politics and influence peddling."</u>
by J. Wright

Failure to pass the so-called Stimulus bill will be a *catastrophe*? So says claims our new president. It's so urgent that our economy may collapse if your grand-kids don't borrow the dollars somewhere to fund these Spending programs? Excuse Me?

I don't see a lot of stimulus, or urgency, in much of the following; all of which are included in Obama's "Stimulus" package, and it isn't bi-partisan in any way, shape or means.

$145 billion for "Making Work Pay" tax credits;
$89 billion for Medicaid; $83 billion for the earned income credit;
$79 billion for State Fiscal Stabilization Fund;
$36 billion for expanded unemployment benefits;
$30 billion for COBRA insurance extension;
$20 billion for food stamps; $15 billion for boosting Pell Grant college scholarships; $15 billion for business-loss carry-backs;
$8 billion for innovative technology loan guarantee program;
$6.2 billion shall be for the Weatherization Assistance Program; $6 billion for university building projects;
$4.5 billion for electricity grid;
$4.5 billion for U.S. Army Corps of Engineers;
$4.2 billion for "neighborhood stabilization activities";
$4 billion for job-training programs, including $1.2 billion to provide "youth" summer jobs for people up to the age of 24;
$3.5 billion for energy efficiency and conservation block grants; for the State Energy Program;
$2.4 billion for carbon-capture; demonstration projects;
$2 billion for federal child care block grants;
$2 billion for renewable energy research;
$2 billion for a "clean-coal" power plant in Illinois.

Those items are merely a portion of the total bill.

Syndicated columnist Charles Krauthammer wrote: *"(Obama was elected) to create something new -- a new politics where the moneyed pork-barreling and corrupt logrolling of the past would give way to a bottom-up, grass-roots participatory democracy. That is what made Obama so dazzling and new."*

Instead, folks, we're getting "perhaps the greatest frenzy of old-politics influence peddling ever seen in Washington." This is not the "Change" I expected.

Krauthammer source: *http://www.washingtonpost.com/wp-dyn/content/article/2009/02/05/AR2009020502766_pf.html*

Thanks for your time, Jaq

Monday, February 9, 2009

A Stone Deaf Senate vs. the People's Will?

by J. Wright

The U.S. Senate is poised to vote and pass a humungous non-stimulus bill that according to the latest Rasmussen poll, 62 % of U.S. voters want the plan to include <u>more tax cuts and less government spending</u>. Only 14% would like it to move in the opposite direction.

Unfortunately, the majority isn't being heard this time around except by 216 Republicans and 11 House Democrats who thus far are against it. It's a (Obama-Reid-Pelosi) Democrat bill.

A few days ago the Congressional Budget Office (CBO), the Senate's "watch dog," claimed that this overstuffed bill would do more damage in the end than it would help. According to even the best Democrat sources, this pork-laden bill will only create about 1.3 million jobs at best; that at a huge cost of more than $120,000 dollars per job according to one Senator, and all at our grandkids expense. Well, boys and girls, the U.S. Treasury doesn't have $815 billion spare dollars in it so the money will have to be borrowed and paid back eventually by someone. None of this has changed any Democrat Senator's mind.

Several months ago when the so-called "Comprehensive Immigration Bill" was placed before the Senate, the people made it abundantly clear that this was <u>not</u> what they wanted. Upon hearing that loud and clear, the Senate let the bill die. This go-round, with a Democrat controlled Senate and House, it's fat city and our future taxpayers, our grand-kids, who are going to pay the bill? I find that unconscionable and highly irresponsible.

I'm a conservative that is all for seeing President Obama succeed, <u>as long as what he espouses is for the greater good of the country.</u> If it's only an expensive, wasteful measure to ensure that his party and those elected representatives in it succeed and gain in political power, then count me out.

Thanks for your time, Jaq

Thursday, February 12, 2009

"Stealth Health?" If not, just call it Socialized Medicine

by J. Wright

Candidate Obama campaigned on the premise that all America would access the same health coverage that he and others in Congress enjoy. Wrong!

If the current pork-filled "Stimulus Plan" leaves the Congressional Conference Committee intact, count on socialized healthcare stealthily becoming law because president Obama's "Stimulus Plan" contains an unprecedented federal takeover of our current healthcare system.

According to Betsy McCaughey, former lieutenant governor of New York state, here is some of what Obama and Company have in store, especially for those of us who are seniors:

Your current medical records, retrieved from your doctor or hospital, will be tracked electronically on a national database to be monitored and tracked to make sure they agree with what Washington, D.C. deems effective and necessary. The new system is compulsory -- doctors and hospitals who are not "meaningful users" will be forced to pay penalties.

A new Health Czar - a "National Coordinator of Health Information" – will oversee the system. The bill establishes something called the "Federal Coordinating Council for Comparative Effectiveness Research" that will ultimately establish what procedures are "effective." A federal HMO in other words.

A dangerous standard of cost effectiveness will be added to the Medicare equation, which could lead to health rationing among the elderly for whom expensive treatments are less cost-effective. A senior can out live the benefit, in essence meaning that you will be considered too old for further treatments. Good luck. Maybe Good-bye.

This bill will affect every part of healthcare: how patients are treated and how much hospitals are paid. This "stealth health" bill allocates more funding for this new bureaucracy than for the Army, Navy, Marines and Air Force combined.

European style socialized healthcare - attempted more than a decade ago by Hillary Clinton and thrown out, now masterminded by socialist strategists months ago and sneaked into the "stimulus" bill – may become law. Thank you Tom Daschle, who didn't become Secretary of HUD but did write this proposal into the "Stimulus Plan." As an Obama staffer indicated in a TV interview, *"This is what the voters asked for."* It isn't what Obama promised.

Thanks for your time, Jaq

Tuesday, February 17, 2009
Are our Michigan Legislators Becoming Too Elitist?
by J. Wright

In a recent article published in the Cadillac News, from the Oakland Press, Pontiac, Senate Majority Leader Mike Bishop, R-Rochester, proposed that legislative term limits *(implemented by the voters in*

1992) should be rescinded because the state lawmakers don't have time to do the people's business.

Their top priority, running for reelection, takes up too much of their time. Doing the people's business came in a distant fourth.

It's my understanding that their "top priority" should be tending to the people's business: by representing and governing. For that they are paid a healthy $79,650.00 base salary *(the second highest in the nation for state legislators)* plus benefits and perquisites; all that for investing about 800 hours annually, or about 20 normal workweeks. They refer to that as "full-time," and in doing so, Michigan is one of eleven states that have a full-time legislature. Additionally, if they serve for six years they are eligible to receive full pay at retirement.

Bishop also proposes that the legislature only serve "half-time." It appears that's the case already. Would his proposal also cut their salaries and benefits in half? The article didn't say.

If our legislators haven't the time to tackle and solve the steep learning curve in Lansing, and if running for reelection actually is their "top priority" upon taking office, then we voters elected the wrong people.

As far as rescinding legislative term limits, it was reported a few weeks ago that 2/3 of the Michigan voters still approved of them, so why should we sit back and allow a few legislators in Lansing to overturn the voter's will, especially when it requires amending the constitution?

Perhaps an overhaul is needed, perhaps more drastic actions than Senator Bishop had in mind. Like others, I'm in favor of disbanding the State Senate altogether and forming a smaller, unicameral legislature limited to a six month annual session. That would be a start.

Thanks for your time, Jaq

Saturday, February 21, 2009

Talk about the foxes guarding the hen house.

by J. Wright

I read an interesting piece on the <u>Wall Street Journal.com</u> web site written by Liz Peek where she stated that President Obama's first month in office had been graded an "F" by the folks on Wall Street. Certainly, the Dow Jones Industrial averages have plunged drastically and the economy hasn't improved even with the billion upon billions being stoked into it via "Stimulus", but can it all be Obama's fault?

Any more than what he inherited and continually blames on former President Bush is Bush's fault?

If presidents had the power to turn our national economy around, why didn't Jimmy Carter do it in the 1970s instead of allowing the quagmire that Ronald Reagan inherited to transpire? If presidents can do so much and be so powerful, why didn't President Bill Clinton alter the direction of the economy at the end of his second term of office?

In 2000, George W. Bush inherited what was rightly Clinton's recession, but the biased mainstream media and the Democrat politicians quickly blamed the previously weakening economy on Bush, as "failed Bush policies."

Today, with the Democrats having been in control of federal spending since 2006, none of what has taken place since Obama's nomination and election has stuck to him; it's still being blamed on Bush. I find it dazzling that the stream can flow in both directions simultaneously. It must totally confuse the fish.

Much of this gigantic problem actually began in 1977 when Jimmy Carter who with the aid of the Democratic legislature enacted the <u>Community Reinvestment Act</u> *(CRA, a favorite target of mine)*, which forced financial institutions to lend mortgage money to questionable applicants who lived in questionable neighborhoods, all in the name of "Affordable Housing." Fannie Mae and Freddie Mac guaranteed a lot of that money and you can see where that got us. Now today, it's more precious tax dollars going to bail out some of those mortgage loans *(and to prop up Freddie and Fannie)*.

Ignoring early warnings from the Bush Administration and even Senator John McCain, Democrats Barney Frank and Chris Dodd, with the support of the Congressional Black Caucus, claimed that these two financial institutions were lily-white in their dealings. Today those two chair important legislative committees overseeing our economy and contribute to 'Obama-nomics,' or, the fox guarding the hen house.

Essentially, many of the same people that helped to create this tremendous financial mess are the ones in charge of fixing it. If this is a form of "Job Security," I think it stinks to high heaven. "Change" definitely is necessary.

Thanks for your time, Jaq

Tuesday, March 3, 2009

More Hypocrisy from Our Shameless Media

J. Wright

Some homework may have been in order for the individual who wrote in the Cadillac News recently bemoaning the "plight" of Henrietta Hughes. Mrs. Hughes, the elderly black, alleged homeless, unemployed woman, sat front row center directly in front of President Obama at a recent town hall meeting in Fort Myers Florida and claimed to be living in her pickup truck with her son. Getting his attention, she soulfully asked the President for a house so she could have her own kitchen and bathroom.

Chene Thompson, wife of Republican State Representative Nick Thompson stepped forward. "Basically," she said, "I offered Ms. Hughes and her son the opportunity to stay in my home rent free for as long as they need to. I'm not a millionaire, I'm not rich, but this is what I can do for someone if they need it." Somehow the main stream media gave President Obama credit for Chene Thompson's charity.

Then the truth came out. *(Ouch!)* Henrietta Hughes is not the homeless disadvantaged person she claimed to be and the media knows it, but instead of admitting that she was a mere shill for the Obama public relations team, they faithfully chose to ignore the facts.

The following, taken from the liepolitic.com web site makes it perfectly clear: *"The hypocrisy of the liberal media speaks for itself. Henrietta has been shown to be a complete fraud and the media has silenced their praise. Do they point out their blunder? Do they admit that Obama staged a lie? Do any of them have the courage to admit their headlines were total distortions?*

It hasn't happened because they want you to forget. They know Obama lied. They lied. They know that you know they lied. Sad isn't it?"

It is sad. It's sadder when good folks are duped into believing a blatant lie. One staged purely for political advantage.

Thanks for your time, Jaq

Friday, March 6, 2009

"Health, education and energy -- worthy and weighty as they may be-- are not the cause of our financial collapse."

by J. Wright

If you currently have a 401-k investment, a mutual funds account, or any of dozens of other investments in our stock market, you are probably like many ordinary Americans; not filthy rich but at some point had some extra dollars to stash away beyond your annual budget requirements, maybe for your retirement years. If so, you are acutely aware that since November 4, the day when candidate Obama was elected to the highest office in the land, the value of the stock market and your investments have shrunk about 31% in value; or in total dollars, about $3-trillion dollars in lost investments.

President Obama recently sloughed off those stock market losses, likening them to a political "tracking poll" that fluctuates up and down. *(In this case, it has all been down.)* Those financial loses of yours mean nothing. In other words, your dollar investment is now worth about 69-cents. In order to counter that, the Obama White House is currently attacking radio personality Rush Limbaugh. Where are the adults?

So what is the newest, gimmicky, dishonest solution emanating from the Obama White House think tank? Instead of coming up with a feasible, workable plan to rescue our deteriorating banking system and possibly stop the downward slide of the markets, he's now blaming the nation's ongoing financial problems on our inability to provide improvements to national health, education, and energy.

As veteran journalist, Charles Krauthammer recently wrote: *"Clever politics, but intellectually dishonest to the core. Health, education and energy -- worthy and weighty as they may be -- are not the cause of our financial collapse. And they are not the cure. The fraudulent claim that they are both cause and cure is the rhetorical device by which an ambitious president intends to enact the most radical agenda of social transformation seen in our lifetime."*

Candidate Obama campaigned on "Change." I wonder now, after a mere six weeks since his inauguration, how many of the Obama faithful are experiencing buyer's remorse.

Krauthammer Quote Source:
http://www.realclearpolitics.com/articles/2009/03/a_dishonest_gim micky_budget.html.

Then there was this headline from the Internet today:
Since President Obama took the oath of office, The Dow Jones Industrial Average has fallen 20 percent

Friday, March 06, 2009--The Dow Jones Industrial Average has fallen faster under President Obama than under any new president in at least 90 years, according to a review conducted by Bloomberg percent, leading at least one investor to dub this the "Obama bear market."

The Dow has also dropped 31 percent since Election Day. Despite a string of government bailout offers and Obama's advice earlier this week that Americans should be buying stock while shares are low, the Dow has continued to freefall.

Bloomberg reported that Obama is at risk of breaking a historical trend -- in which the Dow soars an average of close to 10 percent in the first year after a Democrat wins the presidency. Business reacts to policy and you are seeing that reaction to the largest budget and government takeover of private industry in U.S. History

Thanks for your time, Jaq

Wednesday, March 18, 2009

Voter Outrage Has Its Place; Ignoring the Constitution? Never!

by J. Wright

The American International Group, known familiarly as AIG, has generated some great headlines lately along with much self-righteous braggadocio emitting from many of our elected politicians in Washington, D.C. including our new president, Barack Obama. The latest brouhaha involving AIG stems from its paying out of $165 million in executive bonuses; bonuses that purportedly were part of previous contract agreements between AIG and some of their top-level employees.

Politicians of all stripes in Washington, including many ordinary taxpayers who get their news spoon fed via the "main stream media," became outraged. Sadly, the outrage coming from Washington is a theatrical sham: the politicians knew about AIG's proposed bonus payments weeks ago because it was written quite plainly in the "Stimulus Bill" supported earlier by nearly every elected Democrat in both legislative branches and enacted with President Obama's signature.

Some of the politicians screaming the loudest are those who previously received huge sums of campaign cash from AIG before the economic collapse began, namely Senator Chris Dodd, D-CN. Now they are "outraged" at the behavior of one that has fed them.

Beyond that, others of the outraged legislators have proposed ill-considered legislation *(Read: Illegal)* seeking to force AIG employees who received the taxpayer bonus dollars to return it. I'd suggest the legislators read the U.S. Constitution first, beginning with this: A **Bill of Attainder** is an act of legislature declaring a person or group of persons guilty of some crime and punishing them without benefit of a trial. Article I, section 9, clause 3 of the U.S.

Constitution forbids Bills of Attainder.

Yet an outstate New York Democrat member of the U.S. House of Representatives is hell-bent on defying the Constitution. "I think it's legal," she said. "Contracts get broken and rewritten all the time." Good grief! I have two questions: where do these people come from? Who elects these people? Voter outrage certainly has its place. Ignoring the Constitution is never acceptable.

For more interesting info regarding AIG's generous contribution to candidate Obama's presidential campaign, visit the following link: *http://www.examiner.com/x-268-Right-Side-Politics-Examiner~y2009m3d17-Obama-Received-a-101332-Bonus-from-AIG*

Thanks for your time, Jaq

Tuesday, March 24, 2009

More Discussion on the Henrietta Hughes Poverty Hoax

by J. Wright

My good friend Tom wrote in today's Cadillac News and chided me, asking in essence if the information *(theliepolitic.com)* I posted as a source for the Henrietta Hughes poverty hoax was verifiable.

Henrietta Hughes, you may remember, was the elderly black woman, allegedly poor and unemployed, who sat front-row center at a Fort Myers Florida town hall meeting, which hosted President Obama.

Henrietta gave a sterling performance in front of our president and the live TV cameras as she pleaded for a home of her own so she could have a kitchen and a bathroom because she and her son were living in a pickup truck.

Front-row center was also where several supporters of Candidate Obama were seated at various other campaign stops where they either fainted or swooned during his recitations from the ever-present Teleprompters and were "rescued" by the artful candidate who just happened to have some bottled water handy enough to toss down to them. All of these coincidences constantly happen in real life, of that I'm certain. But I digress, let's move along.

I'd invite my good friend Tom to visit *theliepolitic.com,* or an Internet search engine of his choice, and read what others have to say beyond what I previously posted here and on blogspot.com.

Apparently, Henrietta is, or has been, a successful real estate investor who became "homeless" when she quitclaimed her property over to her son, Corey. That information was also picked up by *redcounty.com,* another Internet web source in an article written by Rus Thompson on February 23, stating: *"Just as I and so many others suspected, this poor woman was a plant. Either that or she is the dumbest real estate investor on the planet, but at the same time, she blew all that cash? Shifted it all into her poor son's name."*

Thompson's article furnishes recent property transactions of Henrietta. According to Lee County, Florida property records, she signed a quitclaim deed in 2006, giving total ownership of a $124,000 valued residential property to her son Corey Lamont. Red county Journalist Rus Thompson went on to say, *"I would guess this is because the value of the property would affect SSDI benefits along with Medicare/Medicaid."*

Further research of property records found that Henrietta Hughes owned as many as three different homes in recent years. Was she a plant; a shill? Was I being disingenuous as my friend Tom suggested? Pffft! Decide for yourself.

Henrietta Hughes was the story the Obama staffers wanted out in the public eye in order to push for more social engineering legislation. The starry-eyed Mainstream Media bought into Henrietta hook, line and sinker, UNTIL the truth came out. Then she quickly became a non-story. How typical of the MSM and their intense task of carrying this administration's water. My post took on the media for being complicit in deceit.

Rus Thompson, Redcounty.com source: *http://redcounty.com/sarasota/2009/02/obamas-homeless-fort-myers-wom*

Thanks for your time, Jaq

Sunday, March 29, 2009

"Why I No Longer Support the War"

A GUEST ARTICLE submitted by J.B.

(J.B. is an Internet friend of mine going back several years. She resides in New England and loves it! In this article, she speaks from her heart in a clear, articulate manner. No Teleprompters were required.)

... ...

Over the course of the last 60 plus days, we have been treated to quite a spectacle out of Washington, D.C. and none of it pretty or encouraging but most of it enlightening. We have buffoons and their jesters in charge of our government, and try as the people might, these same buffoons and jesters have blinders on and no longer see the outrage of the American people.

That they salivate and slip on their own detritus clamoring to squeeze the very last breath out of common sense and common decency is becoming more than just a sideshow; the main event. That's too bad for the people, it's too bad for our form of government and it's too bad for the Nation as a whole.

Oh, yes, we've heard, false as it is, about how the poor the vast unwashed poor have suffered over the centuries of our Nation's existence and it's time to right the wrongs and set the records straight taking the ill-gotten gains of hard working Americans who succeed and produce and give those rewards to the vast unwashed poor who have suffered over the centuries of our Nation's existence. That the exercise would be laudable if the circumstances were true is just a side show.

So, what we are treated to of late is the disassembling of not only the character of who we are as a Nation but the very fiber of what we as a Nation are made of, what we believe and how we get to where we want to go as a person, as a people and as a Nation.

The success of our Nation and the producers and the earners who create that success is being called into question worldwide. That we have become a Nation of ideologues with no direction to succeed but to destroy is very clear to even the most blinded in our country and especially worldwide. Because our success as a Nation is being called into question, we are about to lose our status as a solid investment for the future, our dollar which once was the currency the world used as a basis for valuing commodities worldwide is being called into question and could very well change. Our banks are ridiculed , demoralized and 'scapegoated'.

And who suffers? The people and that includes the fake poor, the vast unwashed poor who have suffered over the centuries of our Nation's existence, that this government intends to raise up, not because they have earned the merit to be raised up by their own hard work and tenacity but on the backs of earners and producers. Unfortunately for this government those earners and producers aren't earning and producing.

What I've just rendered is the template for the insanity coming out of Washington, D.C. and this government. Now, let's expand on that insanity.

So far, we've been talking about rights and monetary inconsistencies and a philosophy permeating Washington that is bogus, ridiculous and useful only in expanding government and nothing more. But underneath it all and hidden far away from sight is a War on Terror that we have been engaged in and the name of which we shall not be permitted to mention ever again.

That which we shall not be permitted to mention ever again involves the lives of our sons and daughters and fathers and mothers who answer the call of a Nation to serve.
If this government is so cavalier in its handling of the future of our children not born yet by saddling them with a debt they could never pay within their lifetimes, we should not expect an attitude and ideological mindset that is different for our children and our family members serving in our Military.

We no longer refer to the War on Terror as a war but some "Man-made gibberish" according to the dictates of Janet Napolitano, the Homeland Security Czar. We no longer refer to the enemy we are fighting as enemy combatants. We no longer have a clear and defining mission in Afghanistan but we are accelerating troop deployment. We are told that the same philosophy and tactics used to win in Iraq will be used in Afghanistan without taking into account that we are talking about two different types of countries, governments and people.

We are releasing prisoners from Guantanamo and relocating them to the United States and providing them shelter instead of repatriating them back to where they came from before they took up arms against our Military and against this Nation.

In less than three months in office, Obama has not become Jimmy Carter by using the same economic thinking he used. He has reached back even further to Lyndon B. Johnson and his template for redistributing wealth by tweaking the "Great Society" and the failed "War on Poverty." Most importantly, however, Obama has reached back to Johnson's escalation of troops in Vietnam with no mission philosophy behind them except the title of "advisor." Obama has 'Vietnamized' the unnamed and unmentionable War on Terror. We are not going back to pre-9/11, we're going to 1965.T

Therefore, I can no longer support the unnamed. That I will continue to support the men and women assigned to the nebulous task of advisor and training in Afghanistan during an unnamed exercise is without question. But I aggressively support their return home immediately.

The blood, sweat, tears and the very lives of our sons and daughters and husbands and wives are far too valuable for this government to squander as if they are nothing more than the pieces of silver already being thrown away.

... ...

Thanks, JB, -- Thanks for your time, Jaq

Saturday, April 11, 2009

The Hypocrisy of Liberal Socialism Laid Bare

J. Wright says, "This is one of the best descriptions of the Hypocrisy of Liberal Socialism I've ever read. *If only we knew who wrote it. Enjoy!*"

There was a time in recent American history when certain Soviet jokes didn't work in translation - not so much because of the language differences, but because of the lack of common sociopolitical context. But that is changing. As President Obama is preparing us for a great leap towards collectivism, I find myself recollecting forgotten political jokes I shared with comrades while living in the old country under Brezhnev, Andropov, and Gorbachev. *(I was too young to remember the Khrushchev times, but I remember the Khrushchev jokes.)* I also noticed that the further America "advances" back to the Soviet model, the more translatable the old Soviet jokes become.

Not all Soviet advancements have metastasized here yet, but we have nearly four more glorious years in which to make it happen. One of my favorite Russian political jokes was this, the six dialectical contradictions of socialism in the USSR:

There is full employment - yet no one is working.
No one is working - yet the factory quotas are fulfilled.
The factory quotas are fulfilled - yet the stores have nothing to sell.
The stores have nothing to sell - yet people got all the stuff at home.
People got all the stuff at home - yet everyone is complaining.
Everyone is complaining - yet the voting is always unanimous.
It reads like a poem - only instead of the rhythm of syllables and rhyming sounds, it's the rhythm of logic and rhyming meanings. If I could replicate it, I might start a whole new genre of "contradictory six-liners." It would be extremely difficult to keep it real and funny at the same time, but I'll try anyway.

Dialectical contradictions are one of the pillars in Marxist philosophy, which states that contradictions eventually lead to a unity of opposites as the result of a struggle. This gave a convenient "scientific" excuse for the existence of contradictions in a socialist society, where opposites were nice and agreeable - unlike the wild and crazy opposites of capitalism that could never be reconciled. Hence the joke. Then I moved to America, where wild and crazy opposites of capitalism were supposedly at their worst. Until recently, however, the only contradictions that struck me as irreconcilable were these:

Economic justice:
America is capitalist and greedy - yet half of the population is subsidized.
Half of the population is subsidized - yet they think they are victims.
They think they are victims - yet their representatives run the government.
Their representatives run the government - yet the poor keep getting poorer.
The poor keep getting poorer - yet they have things that people in other countries only dream about.
They have things that people in other countries only dream about - yet they want America to be more like those other countries.

Hollywood clichés:
Without capitalism there'd be no Hollywood - yet Hollywood dislikes capitalism.
Hollywood dislikes capitalism - yet they sue for unauthorized

copying of movies.
They sue for unauthorized copying - yet on screen they teach us to share.
On screen they teach us to share - yet they keep their millions to themselves.
They keep their millions to themselves - yet they revel in stories of American misery and depravity.
They revel in stories of American misery and depravity - yet they blame the resulting anti-American sentiment on capitalism. They blame the anti-American sentiment on capitalism - yet capitalism ensures the continuation of a system that makes Hollywood possible.

I never thought I would see socialist contradictions in America, let alone write about them. Somehow, all attempts to organize life according to "progressive" principles always result in such contradictions. And in the areas where "progressives" have assumed positions of leadership - education, news media, or the entertainment industry - contradictions become "historically inevitable."

If one were accidentally to open his eyes and compare the "progressive" narrative with facts on the ground, one might start asking questions. Why, for instance, if the war on terror breeds more terrorists, haven't there been attacks on the U.S. soil since 2001? Why would anyone who supports free speech want to silence talk radio? And why is silencing the opposition called the "Fairness Doctrine"?

After the number of "caring" bleeding-heart politicians in Washington reached a critical mass, it was only a matter of time before the government started ordering banks to help the poor by giving them risky home loans through community organizers:

Which resulted in a bigger demand,
which resulted in rising prices,
which resulted in slimmer chances of repaying the loans,
which resulted in more pressure on the banks,
which resulted in repackaging of bad loans,
which resulted in a collapse of the banks,

which resulted in a recession,
which resulted in many borrowers losing their jobs,
which resulted in delinquent mortgage payments,
which resulted in a financial disaster,
which resulted in a worldwide crisis, with billions of poor people
overseas - who had never seen a community organizer, nor applied
for a bad loan - becoming even poorer than they had been before the
"progressives" in the U.S. government decided to help the poor.

As if that were not enough, the same bleeding hearts are now trying
to fix this by nationalizing the banks so that they can keep issuing
risky loans through community organizers. In other words, to
prevent the toast from landing buttered side down, they're planning
to butter the toast on both sides and hope that it will hover in mid-
air. Which also seems like a sensible alternative energy initiative.

Years ago, moving to America made me feel as though I had
traveled in a time machine from the past. But after the recent
"revolutionary" changes have turned reality on its head - which is
what "revolution" literally means - I'm getting an uneasy feeling I
had come from your future.

As your comrade from the future, I also feel a social obligation to
help my less advanced comrades in the American community, and
prepare them for the transition to the glorious world of underground
literature, half-whispered jokes, and the useful habit of looking over
your shoulder. Don't become a <u>nation of cowards</u> - but watch who
might be listening.

Let's start with these few. People's power:

*Liberals believe they're advancing people's power - yet they don't
believe people can do anything right without government guidance.
People can't do anything right - yet the government bureaucracy can
do everything right.
The government bureaucracy can do everything - yet liberals don't
like it when the government takes control of their lives.
Liberals don't like it when the government takes control of their lives
- yet they vote for programs that increase people's dependency on
the government.*

They vote for programs that increase people's dependency on the government - yet they believe they're advancing people's power.

Public education:
Liberals have been in charge of education for 50 years - yet education is out of control.
Education is out of control - yet liberal teaching methods prevail.
Liberal teaching methods prevail - yet public schools are failing.
Public schools are failing - yet their funding keeps growing.
Their funding keeps growing - yet public schools are always underfunded.
Public schools are always underfunded - yet private schools yield <u>better results for less</u>.
Private schools yield better results for less - yet public education is the only way out of the crisis.

One has to believe this author hit the proverbial nail squarely on its head! Amen!

Thanks for your time, Jaq

Tuesday, April 21, 2009

<u>Big Time Corruption Discovered in the Big Federal Bail Outs</u>

by J. Wright

The corruption has begun already. And who would'a thunk it?

Last fall you may remember that Bush administration's Secretary of the Treasury Paulson saw a major financial crisis looming and asked Congress, led by liberal Democrats since 2006, to grant him $750 billion in taxpayer dollars to "bail out" various institutions and banks.

According to a recent post in the Baltimore Sun, what started out last October as a single-purpose $750 billion effort to buy toxic securities has now, under President Obama and the spend-happy Democrat Congress morphed into 12 separate programs that covers up to $3 trillion in direct spending, loans and loan guarantees. The program has now committed an amount equal to the entire annual federal budget.

Bush's Treasury Secretary Paulson spent half of the original $750 billion. President Obama's Treasury Secretary Timothy Geithner *(the same guy who earlier failed to pay his federal taxes in full and now heads up the IRS)* is spending the balance, and more.

Today we have a major disclosure of corruption and fraud in the bailout program according to investigators who have opened 20 criminal probes into possible securities fraud, tax law violations, insider trading and mortgage modification fraud. The chief investigator indicated that the investigations are just the first wave of cases by his office. He expects criminal indictments to occur later this year. He added that ultimately, the fraud could run into the tens of billions of dollars and the risk of those kinds of criminal activities is growing as the bailout becomes bigger and more complex.

The original $750 billion seems small now compared to the multi-trillions of taxpayer dollars the Obama Administration has proposed in further bailouts and reckless spending. The Treasury Department was asked to abandon its current proposed method of buying certain toxic assets. Treasury responded saying it would "consider" the request. Apparently, corruption is no big deal.

How will it end? How many taxpayer dollars will find their way into the wrong pockets?

Thanks for your time, Jaq

Tuesday, April 28, 2009

More Attacks from the Left on our Constitution

by J. Wright.

Recently the U.S Senate entertained a bill, which would allow President Obama to shut down the Internet in the event of a national emergency. A Zogby poll afterward reflected that 81 % of those polled were in opposition with only 5% in favor of such a drastic move.

Another rights infringing bill that could pass the U.S. House this week would outlaw preaching against homosexuality, calling it a "Hate Crime." What happened to the First amendment of our Constitution allowing Freedoms of Religion and Expression?

Or should we consider Homeland Security Secretary Janet Napolitano's recent controversial report to our nation's law enforcement officials to be looked at as a Hate Crime as well, not to mention the continuing vitriolic blasts aimed at Alaska's Governor Sarah Palin and her family by the extreme leftists, especially MSNBC Cable News and the mainstream press? I mean they are mere words, similar to those the House bill would label as Hate Crimes.

Fair is fair. What Congress is attempting is far worse than an Evangelist Pastor or layperson expressing an opinion, which the last time I looked, the First Amendment still protected.

Maybe the next set of laws our Democrat Congress will consider might eliminate the open practice of Christianity altogether, making its practice punishable. What a wonderful new world we're living in today, so full of "Change."

President Obama has been in office 100 days or so and he had an opportunity, as did former President Clinton, to work wonders. Instead he is caving to the radical leftists in his party, who in my opinion, seem hell-bent on driving America's government in the direction of progressive socialism, or worse. I'm not certain this is the "Change" many of his supporters had in mind, certainly not what the Founding Fathers of our Republic had in mind. Pray folks.

Thanks for your time, Jaq

Thursday, April 30, 2009

Obama's Grand Plan to Spend Us Into Prosperity

J. Wright says; "This is not an original of mine. It's an article based on a recent <u>Fact Check.com</u> report and well worth repeating."

FACT CHECK.org:
Obama disowns deficit he helped shape
Apr 29, 5:55 PM (ET)By CALVIN WOODWARD

WASHINGTON (AP) - "That wasn't me," Barack Obama said on his 100th day in office, disclaiming responsibility for the huge budget deficit waiting for him on Day One. It actually was him - and the other Democrats controlling Congress the previous two years - who shaped a budget so out of balance.

And as a presidential candidate and president-elect, he backed the twilight Bush-era Stimulus Plan that made the deficit deeper, all before he took over and promoted spending plans that have made it much deeper still.

Obama met citizens at an Arnold, MO, high school Wednesday in advance of his prime-time news conference. Both forums were a platform to review is progress at the 100-day mark and look ahead.

At various times, he brought an air of certainty to ambitions that are far from cast in stone. His assertion that his proposed budget "will cut the deficit in half by the end of my first term" is an eyeball-roller among many economists, given the uncharted terrain of trillion-dollar deficits and economic calamity that the government is negotiating.

He promised vast savings from increased spending on preventive healthcare in the face of doubts that such an effort, however laudable it might be for public welfare, can pay for itself, let alone yield huge savings.

A look at some of his claims:

OBAMA: "Number one, we inherited a $1.3 trillion deficit ... that wasn't me. Number two, there is almost uniform consensus among economists that in the middle of the biggest crisis, financial crisis, since the Great Depression, we had to take extraordinary steps. So you've got a lot of Republican economists who agree that we had to do a stimulus package and we had to do something about the banks. Those are one-time charges, and they're big, and they'll make our deficits go up over the next two years."

THE FACTS: *Congress controls the purse strings, not the president, and it was under Democratic control for Obama's last two years as Illinois senator. Obama supported the emergency bailout package in President George W. Bush's final months - a package Democratic leaders wanted to make bigger.*

To be sure, Obama opposed the Iraq war, a drain on federal coffers for six years before he became president. But with one major exception, he voted in support of Iraq war spending.

The economy has worsened under Obama, though from forces surely in play before he became president, and he can credibly claim to have inherited a grim situation. Still, his response to the crisis goes well beyond "one-time charges."

He's persuaded Congress to expand children's health insurance, education spending, health information technology and more. He's moving ahead on a variety of big-ticket items on healthcare, the environment, energy and transportation that, if achieved, will be more enduring than bank bailouts and aid for homeowners.

The nonpartisan Committee for a Responsible Federal Budget estimated his policy proposals would add a net $428 billion to the deficit over four years, even accounting for his spending reduction goals. Now, the deficit is nearly quadrupling to $1.75 trillion.

OBAMA: "I think one basic principle that we know is that the more we do on the (disease) prevention side, the more we can obtain serious savings down the road ... If we're making those investments, we will save huge amounts of money in the long term."

THE FACTS: *It sounds believable that preventing illness should be cheaper than treating it, and indeed that's the case with steps like preventing smoking and improving diets and exercise. But during the 2008 campaign, when Obama and other presidential candidates were touting a focus on preventive care, the New England Journal of Medicine cautioned that "sweeping statements about the cost-saving potential of prevention, however, are overreaching." It said that, "Although some preventive measures do save money, the vast majority reviewed in the health economics literature do not."*

And a study released in December by the Congressional Budget Office found that increasing preventive care "could improve people's health but would probably generate either modest reductions in the overall costs of healthcare or increases in such spending within a 10-year budgetary time frame."

OBAMA: "You could cut (Social Security) benefits. You could raise the tax on everybody so everybody's payroll tax goes up a little bit. Or you can do what I think is probably the best solution, which is you can raise the cap on the payroll tax."

THE FACTS: *Obama's proposal would reduce the Social Security trust fund's deficit by less than half, according to the nonpartisan Tax Policy Center. That means he would still have to cut benefits,* *raise the payroll tax rate, raise the retirement age or some combination to deal with the program's long-term imbalance.*

Workers currently pay 6.2 percent and their employers pay an equal rate - for a total of 12.4 percent - on annual wages of up to $106,800, after which no more payroll tax is collected.

Obama wants workers making more than $250,000 to pay payroll tax on their income over that amount. That would still protect workers making under $250,000 from an additional burden. But it would raise much less money than removing the cap completely.

Associated Press writers Kevin Freking and Jim Kuhnhenn contributed to this report.

Thanks for your time, Jaq

Friday, May 8, 2009

Will Michigan's Stimulus Billions Be Rescinded Too?

by J. Wright

A couple of weeks ago the Detroit News reported that the State House Republican leaders in Lansing were pressuring Democrat Governor Jennifer Granholm to slash state spending another half-billion dollars because revenue is falling short by $25 million a week.

The Republicans suggested that Granholm could accomplish the spending cuts by reducing all governmental department's wages by 5 percent across-the-board; a 5-percent wage cut for Michigan's 52,000 state workers and a 5-percent increase in the amount state workers must contribute for healthcare coverage.

They also called for 5-percent cuts in lawmakers' office budgets, pay for non-teaching workers at the fifteen public universities and pay for legislative employees. It wasn't mentioned if the state lawmakers, the second highest paid in the nation, would accept a wage cut as well.

This should be interesting to watch. The Los Angeles Times has reported that the Obama administration is threatening to rescind billions of dollars in federal stimulus money to California if liberal Republican Governor Arnold Schwarzenegger and state lawmakers do not restore wage cuts to unionized home healthcare workers approved in February as part of the budget. California, much like Michigan, only worse off financially, has a tremendous budget deficit currently with no seeming resolution in sight.

Like California, many of Michigan's state workers fall in the category as union members. Will Obama's Administration threaten fellow Democrat Governor Jennifer Granhom with rescinding the billions of "stimulus" dollars promised to Michigan now? Or, because she is a Democrat, will they simply look the other way if Michigan's state workers are forced to accept a cut?

I'm semi-curious as to how many of our state workers might have voted for both Obama and Granholm and are wondering why today. Like I said, this should be interesting to watch.

Thanks for your time, Jaq

Wednesday, May 20, 2009

A Letter from a Dodge Dealer, soon to be "former dealer."

by J. Wright

For all the supporters of President Obama and his Administration currently intent on socializing or destroying privately owned businesses, some very much like Don's Auto Clinic, or Godfrey Chevrolet-Buick, here in Cadillac, MI , or that of a personal life-long friend, *(James)* McHugh Dodge-Jeep in Zanesville, OH.

Please read on...

May 19, 2009 – a Letter to the Editor from a Dodge dealer:

My name is George C. Joseph. I am the sole owner of Sunshine Dodge-Isuzu, a family owned and operated business in Melbourne, Florida. My family bought and paid for this automobile franchise 35 years ago in 1974. I am the second generation to manage this business.

We currently employ 50+ people and before the economic slowdown we employed over 70 local people. We are active in the community and the local chamber of commerce. We deal with several dozen local vendors on a day to day basis and many more during a month. All depend on our business for part of their livelihood. We are financially strong with great respect in the market place and community. We have strong local presence and stability.

I work every day the store is open, nine to ten hours a day. I know most of our customers and all our employees. Sunshine Dodge is my life.

*On Thursday, May 14, 2009 I was notified that my **Dodge franchise**, that we purchased, will be taken away from my family on June 9, 2009 **without compensation and given to another dealer at no cost to them.** My new vehicle inventory consists of 125 vehicles with a financed balance of 3 million dollars. This inventory becomes impossible to sell with no factory incentives beyond June 9, 2009. Without the Dodge franchise we can no longer sell a new Dodge as "new," nor will we be able to do any warranty service work.*

Additionally, my Dodge parts inventory, (approximately $300,000.) is virtually worthless without the ability to perform warranty service. There is no offer from Chrysler to buy back the vehicles or parts inventory. We recently totally renovated our facility at Chrysler's insistence, incurring a multi-million dollar debt in the form of a *mortgage at Sun Trust Bank.*

HOW IN THE UNITED STATES OF AMERICA CAN THIS HAPPEN? THIS IS A PRIVATE BUSINESS NOT A GOVERNMENT ENTITY

This is beyond imagination! My business is being stolen from me through NO FAULT OF OUR OWN. We did NOTHING wrong.

This atrocity will most likely force my family into bankruptcy. This will also cause our 50+ employees to be unemployed. How will they provide for their families? This is a total economic disaster.

HOW CAN THIS HAPPEN IN A FREE MARKET ECONOMY IN THE UNITED STATES OF AMERICA?

I beseech your help, and look forward to your reply. Thank you. Sincerely,

George C. Joseph
President & Owner
Sunshine Dodge-Isuzu

Source: <u>American Thinker Blog: Letter from a Dodge dealer</u>

So, welcome to the new 'United Socialist States of America,' boys and girls. "Change You Can Believe In?" I hope the millions of star-stunned idiots that voted for Mr. Obama are discovering that it's not becoming the "Change" they expected.

Thanks for your time, Jaq

Friday, May 22, 2009

Whom to Advise in the Ongoing Israeli-Palestinian Issue

by J. Wright

In reading *Philadelphia Inquirer* columnist and editorial board member Trudy Rubin's recent column in the *Cadillac News*, I found myself amazed at her seeming naiveté in general with the ongoing, never ending Israeli-Palestinian issue.

Ms. Rubin suggested that President Obama "coulda-woulda-shoulda" said things much differently when meeting earlier with Israeli Prime Minister Binyamin Netanyahu at the White House and she offered some examples.

I'm not an expert on mid-east politics either (*a Carpenter by trade actually*) but my memory still works. Obaama's suggestion that Israeli should again seriously recognize a sovereign Palestinian state brings to mind what happened when the Israel government decided to remove itself, its people and military from the contentious Gaza Strip neighboring Egypt. This was a unilateral act on Israel's part to show the Palestinians and their neighboring Arab state supporters that peaceful coexistence might be possible. It takes two to tango.

Israel discovered too late when Hamas, the elected Palestinian terrorist government of the Gaza Strip, began to ruthlessly and indiscriminately shower the neighboring Israeli villages and towns with rockets, killing and injuring hundreds of innocent men, women and children. All while the United Nations looked the other way. Very convenient for Hamas, a declared enemy of Israel who has vowed to never recognize Israel as a Jewish State, or as a sovereign state at all.

I also don't know Israeli Prime Minister Binyamin Netanyahu personally but I'd wager that he is not interested in having a repeat of that mindless behavior coming from the West Bank from a newly formed sovereign Palestinian State. My suggestion would be to not advise Israeli on what to do but instead direct any further discussion at the terrorist government in Gaza, and to any potential Palestinian terrorists in the West Bank. In my biased opinion, that's who requires that proverbial trip to the woodshed.

Lastly, the terrorist government Hamas controls Gaza, and Mahmood Abbas heading the PLO in the West Bank; two Palestinian factions that don't agree on much of anything. How can Obama suggest that Israel make a deal that wouldn't stand a snowball's chance in hell of surviving? To me, in this case it's new math; $1+1+1 = 2$.

Thanks for your time, Jaq

Wednesday, June 10, 2009

Do We Have An Over-reaching Executive Administration?

by J. Wright

Two things in the national political works, at this writing, concern me greatly. One that may become enacted is the proposed appointment by President Obama of an "Executive-Pay Czar," or as sometimes referred to in the media, a "Master of Compensation."

This appointed "Master," not one selected or approved by Congress, will be filled by attorney Kenneth Feinberg, formerly on Vice-president Joe Biden's economic advisory staff. *(Before that, he was in charge of handling the thousands of public donations earmarked for the families of the 9/11 victims and did a good job. He appears occasionally on FOX Cable News as Neil Cavuto's guest).*

Feinberg's job will be to ensure that private companies that received taxpayer bailout dollars from the questionable Troubled Asset Relief Fund (TARP) are abiding by the new executive pay levels put in place by Obama.

To begin with, TARP's constitutionality was highly questionable when the Democrat controlled Congress relinquished its sovereign responsibility for the disbursement of the national treasury to the Executive branch, namely the Secretary of the Treasury under former president Bush and now under Obama. Add to that, the naming of a "Pay Czar" is another affront to the American free enterprise system exercised by the Executive branch whose apparent intention is to control private business expenditures. It's reported that the new federal "Pay Czar's" authority could possibly even reach into private companies that were NOT recipients of TARP. This the America where I grew up? Hardly.

The other issue is how Chrysler Corporation's remaining debt holders had their day before the U.S. Supreme Court and lost, leaving the Indiana Teachers and State Police pensioners funds, whose retirement savings were wrapped up in Chrysler bonds, standing alone in challenging Obama and his administration who earlier had called for "shared sacrifice" in this issue.

As National Review printed recently: "It should be noted that Chrysler's unions, unsecured creditors who jumped to the head of the line thanks to White House power play, did not give an inch on their base pay or pension terms. Who would call that shared sacrifice?"

National Review quote source:
http://planetgore.nationalreview.com/post/?q=ZTA4MTRlYmFiODh hNGU5MDI0YjhhMGNkZTY1NzAwY2Y=.

Thanks for your time, Jaq

Thursday, June 25, 2009

Why This Particular Healthcare Reform Package?

by J. Wright

(Jaq's Note: this blog was my initial mention of what today, in 2014, is called "Affordable Health Care.")

A clever quote from a former U.S Senator, Illinois Republican Everett McKinley Dirksen, who said, *"A million here, a million there, soon adds up to real money."* Not any more, Senator, at least if you are an elected legislator working in Washington, D. C. today.

Remember as recently as last fall when President Bush's Secretary of the Treasury Henry Paulson asked for a then astronomical $700 billion dollars, *($700,000,000,000.00)* which, was eventually approved after much wailing and gnashing of Congressional teeth.

Called TARP for <u>Troubled Asset Relief Program</u>, it expanded beyond the $700 billion before leaving the Senate. Congress entrusted Secretary Paulson, <u>unconstitutionally,</u> to "fix" the financial mess; but it's still with us. Where did the $700 billion in taxpayer dollars go?

Now we are getting used to larger numbers, trillions with 12 zeroes. Dirksen's millions 'here and there', which pale in comparison, is a rounding error in todays D.C. accounting methods.

President Obama started pushing a new healthcare reform package that was to top out at $1 Trillion *(1,000,000,000,000.00)* over ten years. The Congressional Budget Office *(CBO)* took a closer look and came up with $1.6 trillion. Today, their revised figure is $3 trillion. This astronomical amount of future taxpayer debt *(Quoting Obama: 'We don't have the money')* will supposedly provide Americans with a questionable healthcare program similar to that of the UK and Canada, or worse. That's something to look forward to.

Why are we considering this? To provide access or coverage for some unverified number of Americans, who for a multitude of reasons, some personal, do not have health insurance coverage? Even the various plans being considered do not cover everyone, that's been reported for weeks. So how much will this boondoggle really cost if it passes? Many of the legislators are in the dark but are willing to pass the bill anyway. Can "We the People" stop them? Maybe when pigs fly.

We need healthcare reform but is this it?

Thanks for your time, Jaq

Wednesday, July 1, 2009

Step #1 in Totalitarianism - Cap and Trade

by J. Wright

HEADLINE: **Dollar Falls Most in Single Month as China Urges New Reserve Currency.**

That was the June 27 headline at Bloomberg.com, published by the Bloomberg Professional, a service terminal that provides real-time financial news, market data, and analysis. The U.S. Dollar declined the most against the Euro and dropped in value versus the Yen after China challenged Obama-nomics and repeated its call for a new global currency.

What does the decline in value of the dollar mean for you and me? In a capsule, according to the Gerson Lehman Group, its devaluation means higher prices for our everyday goods and commodities, as they are expected to continue to rise along with the value of energy, oil, precious and base metals. Fuel costs will increase, and consumer credit will shrink while inflation increases *(punishing those like me and others on a fixed income).*

The opponents of the president's ominous Cap-and-Trade bill that passed recently in the U.S. House of Representatives said much the same. In the opinion of millions it's a new, unfair tax on energy consumption that will essentially increase the costs of everything we use. Slowdowns in corporate production will ensue. American businesses relocating offshore would result, subsequently followed with the loss of American jobs.

Some politicians say the bill makes sense because if energy costs rise, consumption will be less. The nebulous reasoning is that we'll then lessen our dependence on foreign oil and somehow change our planet's climate. Is this like rearranging the chairs in a restaurant's public smoking section while the growing smoke cloud lingers everywhere? With China and India's growth, the pollution on the planet increases while our cost of living increases and our standard of living erodes, the economy continues to founder, and worse, the central federal government attains more power. We are the losers.

Sources: www.bloomberg.com; www.glgroup.com/

Thanks for your time, Jaq

Wednesday, July 8, 2009
Step #2 in Totalitarianism - Mandatory Home Inspections
by J. Wright-July 8, 2009

So you think "your home is still your castle?" Maybe not if the U.S. Senate actually passes the questionable "Climate" bill the House of Representatives passed last week on a 219-212 vote. It legislates mandatory home inspections by federal government regulators *(Big Brother?)* who will demand to audit every aspect of your home under the threat of substantial and repeated fines if their visits are denied or their demands not satisfied.

(Why does this sound similar to the feds threatening many lenders who were slow to approve questionable mortgage loans made to questionable borrowers?)

The inspectors shall request copies of utility bills, or permission to obtain copies from your utility companies and use them to produce an estimate of generalized end-uses (heating, and cooling); and then will inspect for R-values of wall/ceiling/floor insulation;

- Square footage and approximate age of home;
- Type of windows: glazing type(s) and frame material(s);
- Type, model number, and location of heating/cooling system(s); Type of ductwork, location and R-value of duct insulation, and any indications of previous duct sealing;
- Type of foundation if crawl, basement, or slab;
- Checklist of common air-leakage sites; Estimated age and efficiency of major appliances such as dishwashers, refrigerators, freezers, washers and dryers;
- Number and type of hardwired light fixtures and screw-in bulbs in portable lamps suitable for energy efficient re-lamping;
- Visual indications of condensation; Presence and location of exhaust fans, and whether they are vented outdoors;
- Number and type of water faucets, showerheads; and
- Presence and type(s) of combustion equipment; blocked chimney, and corroded or missing vent connections.

This legislation was fueled on the automatic assumption that Global Warming is taking place and it contributes to rising CO_2 levels, despite the fact that this is a highly contentious question and is being rejected by more and more international scientists, but who cares? Government knows best. If your home doesn't pass muster, what then? Federal fines, or do you spend dollars you can't spare to upgrade?

Information source: *http://www.infowars.com/bureaucrats-will-carry-out-mandatory-home-inspections-under-climate-bill/*

Thanks for your time, Jaq

Wednesday, July 22, 2009

<u>My 2-cents</u>

by J. Wright

Droll Comedian Steven Wright *(not a relative)* once said, "If you get a penny for your thoughts, why do we always put our '2-cents' in?"

<u>Real Politics</u> columnist and FOX Business News analyst, John Stossel, writes on the very confusing issue of national healthcare reform: *"It's crazy for a group of mere mortals to try to design 15% of the U.S. economy. It's even crazier to do it by August. Yet that is what some members of Congress presume to do. They intend, as the New York Times puts it, 'to reinvent the nation's healthcare system.' Let that sink in. A handful of people who probably never ran a small business actually think they can reinvent the nation's healthcare system."*

Stossel gives the congressional legislators credit for being 'mere mortals'. I'd liken them more to being 'arrogant snake-oil salesmen with blown dried hair and good quality suits'. There's an old saying that the definition of an expert is anyone more than 25 miles from home. This appears to be the case of the lawmakers who are attempting to follow President Obama's orders and overhaul *(or possibly ruin?)* our national healthcare system.

From the liberal <u>NY Times</u>:
"Three of the five Congressional committees working on legislation to reinvent the nation's healthcare system delivered bills this week along the lines proposed by President Obama. Instead of celebrating their success, many Democrats were apprehensive, nervous and defensive." That's understandable. Much of what they are proposing is so bizarre that even the unwashed, average American can understand that. Recent national polls reflect it's not to their liking.

The lawmakers can't predict its eventual cost in new taxes, or if it actually improves the system or replaces it with what Canada and the UK currently "enjoy." Still, President Obama is pressing hard for something now. Too often, and unfortunately, what a bill contains is secondary to its passing. This controversial bill will affect *everyone, forever.* Why the rush? Do it right.

Information sources:
http://www.realclearpolitics.com/articles/2009/07/22/arrogance_97 561.html
http://www.nytimes.com/2009/07/18/health/policy/18health.html?_r =3&hp

Thanks for your time, Jaq

Friday, August 14, 2009

Get Ready for Socialized Medicine
by J. Wright

The national healthcare reform proposals being generated in Washington and introduced in Town Hall meetings across the land are not receiving the warm welcome that many politicians wanted or expected. Many ordinary folks in attendance appear to be beyond angry with their lawmakers, who in fact were "hired" at the voting booths to represent but seem hell-bent on passing some sort of radical bill anyway. One, in essence, which *"tears down the house to repair a faucet in the bathroom."* Apparently, the lawmakers are more fearful of their leadership's ability to destroy them than they are of the voters to boot them from office. How else could they all utter the identical pro-reform lines repeatedly?

The bill most discussed, of several being generated, is HR3200, *(please visit: http://www.lc.org/index.cfm?PID=14102&AlertID=10150)* at this point it's a 1,018 page, complicated monstrosity that if passed could result in 30,000 pages of new regulations rivaling our "magnificent" IRS code. That after the government bureaucrats finish fine-tuning and defining it into a total remake of our current medical care system; one that isn't broken but could definitely use some major changes.

The Democrats in power have rejected out-of-hand many changes proposed by Republicans, including tort reform. A major part of the escalating costs of medical care is passed on by the increasing costs of medical malpractice insurance. Anti-tort reform trial lawyers are a major financial contributor to the Democrats. No one wants to close that cash $pigot.

Another tidbit the Democrats refuse to consider is to allow the various independent health insurance companies to sell their wares across state lines. For example, if you live in New York State today and wish to purchase lesser cost insurance in Delaware, you can't.

Why?

Now the Town Hall attendees in disagreement with healthcare reform were accused of being a mob; organized rabble-rousers, etc. because they wanted their voices heard. So the opponents of free speech send in their own 'mob' of organized thugs, even to the point of beating a conservative black man who was handing out "Don't Tread On Me" flags outside one of the town hall meetings. Add to that, Speaker of the House Nancy Pelosi and her political underling, Steny Hoyer, recently labeled public dissent as "un-American." OMG! Our Founding Fathers must be spinning in their graves! And Hillary too?

One line I overheard last week from a Town Hall meeting sticks with me: *"They (the lawmakers) didn't come to listen, they came to teach."*

Good grief! I know all I need to know about any of their various healthcare reform plans, or as Obama now calls it, 'health insurance reform'. What I know is I don't want it! And for all of his so-called oratorical eloquence, President Obama can't explain it short of lying though his teeth about what it includes.

What I fear most is that, come hell-or-high water, these elected idiots, as I mentioned before, are more fearful of Obama's ability to destroy them politically than they are of their constituents booting them out of office. They will dutifully do the bidding of their leader, their *Messiah,* and pass this or a similar abomination, regardless of massive public sentiment to the contrary.

Then what? Wait for the 2010 mid-terms; elect Republican or conservative Independents and attempt feebly to rescind the entire mess with a president holding a veto pen? How much damage will have taken place in the interim.

I sincerely hope that those good folks who were duped into voting for "Change" are choking on their fears right now.

Thanks for your time, Jaq

Saturday, August 22, 2009

Take Care of Federal Deficit Later?

by J. Wright

Friday gave us a "Good news, bad news" scenario: the good news was that President Obama would be vacationing at Martha's Vineyard and out of the public spotlight briefly. *(Or not.)* The bad news is that his administration released a revised report showing the growing federal spending deficit would explode to an outrageous $9 trillion during the next ten years instead of the $7.1 trillion they had projected after taking office. Contrary to the Obama Administration's economic experts, the Congressional Budget Office (CBO) had predicted a $9.1 trillion deficit and it appears they had the right numbers all along. *(Jaq's Note: Wrong, they missed it by almost four years.)*

So for the next ten years our federal government will go along, happily spending $900 billion more dollars annually than it takes in. I wish I could run my household finances like that. Maybe not, come to think of it. The really bad news is this $9 trillion expected deficit increase adds not only to the burgeoning $11.7 trillion National Debt, it doesn't include a single dime for the cost of national health/insurance reform … if somehow passed, would be tacked on.

On May 24, 2009 President Obama, as quoted in the NY Post, said during a lengthy interview referring to the country, "We are out of money, were broke." He also added, as I remember, that our government's current spending habits were "unsustainable."
So what is his solution? Break his campaign promise and increase taxes on every remaining wage earner in order to cover our various near bankrupt social programs? Or, begin to reform all of them, cut wasteful fraud and spending and get our financial house in order before taking on anything new?

Still mired in a deepening recession, and with approximately 30 million currently out of work and growing, a huge amount of social program dollars will never be collected. Scarlett O'Hara might suggest that we "…take care of it tomorrow."

Thanks for your time, Jaq

Friday, September 4, 2009

<u>Why More Pro-healthcare Reform Speeches?</u>

by J Wright

At the risk of sounding anti-Obamacare, whatever that is, it's difficult for me to understand why President Obama, in the face of devastating public opinion to the contrary, insists that a total overhaul of our healthcare system is necessary. Why, if I wanted to replace my kitchen cabinetry and counter tops, would I begin by demolishing the entire house?

Now President Obama is set to make a high-level pitch for healthcare reform before a joint session of Congress. Many of those members, who if brave enough, recently stood before their constituents and felt the heat of an aroused public, which by all national polls, are well satisfied enough with the current system that it doesn't need to be totally destroyed and eventually taken over and operated by the federal government.

President Obama will be preaching to the choir, at least that's how it appears to me. The more he speaks, the faster his job approval ratings plummet, and they have, like a stone. All of his 'face time' on national television has done nothing for health reforms and has definitely affected his popularity. We all know the definition of insanity is to continue doing the same thing and expecting a different result. Mr. President, maybe listening to the people is in order.

Certainly, his failure to get consensus on healthcare reform can't be blamed totally on the Republicans; they have been watching the congressional Democrats doing a good enough job of that.

The House Democrats want a "public option." *(Government run healthcare; eventually eliminating private insurance providers.)* The Senate Democrats say "No" to public option and the Republican Senators are left out of that stalemate all together. Many of their ideas are constructive and bear consideration but the special interests the Democrats favor prohibit even a look-see. No wonder much of the country is upset.

At a televised bi-partisan conference, consisting of the major players in both parties, and headed up by President Obama, Paul Ryan, R-WI, gave a terrific report, which afterward, Obama, looking obviously bored, dismissed merely it as 'talking points.' Pffft! End of unity and any 'across the aisle' compromise. Remember, "I won."

Thanks for your time, Jaq

Friday, September 25, 2009

Now He's Thrown Israel Under the Bus!

by J. Wright

Solely in the spirit of sarcasm, *IF,* in 1948, Israel had never been designated a sovereign nation there would be no 'Mideast problem'.

Or, *IF* Hitler had been better equipped at ridding the world of the 'infestation of Jews' during WW II: same conclusion.

As former Dallas QB "Dandy" Don Meredith once said to sports columnist/announcer Howard Cosell, *"H'ard, if 'ifs and buts' were candy and nuts, what a Merry Christmas we'd all have."*

Going back to the current but incessant, never ending 'Mideast problem', *IF* Jimmy Carter had developed a better pair of gonads as an adolescent, the Mideast would be a far more stable place than it is today. All he can do now, in attempting to cover his skinny, satchel-ass, is blame Israel for everything bad that's ever happened and continue to kiss Muslim ass.

Apparently, President Obama feels that same way. I'm still fuming over his bigoted speech last week at the United Nations general assembly railing at Israel. If I were Bibi Netanyahu, I'd flat knock him on his skinny ass for interfering in the governance of their country. Sure, it would violate untold political decorum but would send a definite message.

Originally, Obama said the 'new' Mideast peace negotiations would commence with no set pre-conditions, then in his usual pseudo-intelligent chin jutting Il Duce fashion, proceeded to lay out several conditions that are, and will be, totally unacceptable to the Israelis. Talk about arrogance. Whose side is he on anyway? I guess we all know now.

Thanks for your time, Jaq

Monday, September 28, 2009

Further Shredding of the Constitution

by J. Wright

After reading a piece in Politico.com, not exactly a radical right-wing web site by any measure, I'm convinced beyond any doubt that the present Obama administration and its fellow lawmakers in D.C. are totally out of their minds. The problem? If this version of Obamacare passes into law and you don't buy mandated health insurance you can be fined, or jailed.

Politico.com published: Sen. John Ensign (R-Nev.) received a handwritten note Thursday from Joint Committee on Taxation Chief of Staff Tom Barthold confirming the penalty for failing to pay the up to $1,900 fee for not buying health insurance. To wit: Violators could be charged with a misdemeanor and could face up to a year in jail or a $25,000 penalty, Barthold wrote it on JCT letterhead. He signed it 'Sincerely, Thomas A. Barthold'.

The note was a follow-up to Senator's Ensign's questioning at the Senate Finance Committee's markup. This is the Committee headed by Senator Max Baucus of Montana. Originally he had a "gang of six," himself, two other Democrat Senators and three deluded Republican Senators, all holed up for several weeks attempting to hammer out what he referred to as a "bipartisan" healthcare reform package.

Apparently, those three deluded Republicans, including a very liberal Olympia Snowe, concluded they were "just for show." When none of their suggestions were accepted by Baucus and the others, they walked. Now Senator Baucus is holding full committee hearings in an attempt to quickly mark up a questionable reform plan that up to now has had about 500 additional amendments added to it *(all submitted by Democrats)*. The old adage about the 'definition of a camel' comes to my mind: A Horse Designed by a Committee.

Yes, we need healthcare/treatment reform; but we don't need to throw the baby out with the bathwater. I totally question the constitutionality of mandating, or forcing citizens to buy anything. Show me where?

Thanks for your time, Jaq

Saturday, October 3, 2009

Now Even the Lawmakers Can't Understand What They Propose...

by J. Wright

In the wee hours of the morning last Friday, the Senate Finance Committee, chaired by Senator Max Baucus, (D-Montana) completed the mark up of their proposed healthcare reform bill.

The committee had been working with a "conceptual" version, or one prepared in common sense language. It had been given in part to their staffers, lawyers, who converted it to legislative language before an upcoming floor vote.

This is a portion of a quote from Senator Tom Carper (D-Del.):
"I don't expect to actually read the legislative language because reading the legislative language is among the more confusing things I've ever read in my life. We, we write in this committee and legislate with plain English and I think most of us can understand most of that. When you get into the legislative language, Senator Conrad actually read some of it, several pages of it the other day and I don't think anybody had a clue--including people who have served on this committee for decades--what he was talking about."

There was more, but perhaps you get the gist. The Senate Finance Committee is the same committee that voted down a proposal to have the bill placed on the Internet 72 hours before an up-down vote takes place on the floor. Senator John F. Kerry, (D-Mass.) indicated it would be too confusing. Was he implying that the average American is too stupid to understand words?

What I don't understand is how the Obama Administration and the leftist Democrat legislators react to national polls concerning the public's seeming disfavor with the Afghanistan conflict, yet totally ignore more conclusive polls concerning widespread opposition to major healthcare overhaul.

Am I one of those average Americans Senator Kerry was speaking about? Maybe so, but I understand words.

Thanks for your time, Jaq

Thursday, October 8, 2009

Debates Won: Wars Lost...

by J. Wright

In a recent Wall Street Journal article, former Bush Administration White House Chief of Staff Karl Rove indicated, *"The GOP is Winning the Health-Care Debate."*

Allow me to take on former tennis great John McEnroe's in-your-face attitude for a second: "Winning the Debate? But Losing the War? You Can't be Serious!"

Great... if that's a victory please excuse me whilst my head explodes!

The Progressive Marxist idiots, whom many of us voted into office, are going to pass their idea of national health reform regardless of rapidly growing public dissatisfaction and the possible political consequences. That's supposed to be a win for the nation?

Once in place, especially with Obama's veto pen until 2012 (or later) their idea of health reform will never be repealed and eventually we'll be "enjoying" a single payer monstrosity similar, maybe worse, than that in the UK and Canada.

It's becoming plain that these power guzzling Progressive Marxists have no conscience when they are in the majority, and in typical liberal fashion, have this inane belief that they and they alone know what is best for the rest of us, the uneducated inferior types.

Sure, many of them will suffer at the polls in 2010 but it's a small price to pay for their cause, as again, they will have forced their will upon us. To put it bluntly, *we've had it.* And I'd love to be wrong.

Additionally, even with the so-called 'pass' the CBO just gave Senator Max Baucus and the Senate Finance Committee's version of national healthcare; the numbers are a joke.

Out of that expected cost of $829-billion spread over ten years, is a huge reduction in Medicare payments to doctors and hospitals of almost half; $404 billion. It's doubtful that will happen. Too many politicians see the folly in screwing with the seniors voting bloc. The additional proposed taxes and fees will certainly take effect but not enough to offset the "savings" in lower Medicare expenses.

Then there's the so-called savings to be garnered by eliminating Medicare "fraud and waste" to the tune of $500 billion? LMAO! As if any Congress after discovering fraud and waste ever did anything about it.

So let's pretend this plan of theirs works for ten years. After that there is no allotment of money on any one's table to maintain this monster entitlement plan. Like now, Medicare/Medicaid is costing ten times what was conceived at its inception 25 or so years ago. Imagine what our kids and their kid's kids will be facing in a couple of decades.

The radical leftists have been compared with an army of ants. Close, only worse. The ants aren't so much interested in control and power as they are in survival of their species.

The leftists will accept a loss of the House in 2010 as long as they pass nationalized healthcare reform now. Like all good socialists, they love their martyrs and are a patient lot. Eventually they would regain the House and control of the taxpayer dollars.

Personally, I don't see a miracle in the making that will prevent them from passing Obamacare, or whatever it's called. And the arrogant One's ego trip will be nauseating to behold when that takes place.

Thanks for your time, Jaq

October 4, 2009

"Trickle Up Economy?"

by J. Wright

Trickle Up Economy? I snicker just thinking about it, sorry... I digress. Presidential hopeful Senator Barack Obama's web site states:

Provide Middle Class Americans Tax Relief...
Obama and Biden will cut income taxes by $1,000 for working families to offset the payroll tax they pay.

Provide a Tax Cut for Working Families:
Obama and Biden will restore fairness to the tax code and provide 150 million workers the tax relief they need. Obama and Biden will create a new "Making Work Pay" tax credit of up to $500 per person, or $1,000 per working family. The "Making Work Pay" tax credit will completely eliminate income taxes for 10 million Americans.

(What about that rhetoric about 'everyone paying their fair share'?)

"Up to" are key words boys and girls, what if it's only $188 depending on your previous year's income. And IF all 150 million workers do receive $500 each in federal welfare, aka "tax relief," where is Obama going to find the money now with the recent brouhaha in D.C. and the huge $700-billion Wall Street bailout? Will he and Joe Biden insist on increasing the federal deficit even more by borrowing the non-existent dollars? Or will they rely on the Fed's printing presses? Certainly, they aren't willing to CUT, or lower, any of the excessive spending they have espoused in their campaign promises. Or to lower their fanciful expectations of what grand social advances they can achieve, at least based on their non-responses in the last two debates when asked a simple question; in these questionable economic times: What of your proposed programs do you intend to eliminate or cut? *(I didn't hear an answer. Did you?)*

As far as "Growing the Economy from the Bottom Up," as they propose, are most of you like me? In my lifetime, every job I ever held was a result of being hired by a profitable businessman, or his personnel manager. I never had a "man on the street" pay my wages. Am I the exception?

Thanks for your time, Jaq

October 19, 2009
<u>EDITOR: Viewpoint/Speak Out</u>
by J. Wright

On August 21, 2008, Democrat presidential candidate Barack Obama said in a televised campaign stop that as president, when it came down to deciding on health care reform that it would be done out in the open with Democrats, Republicans, Independents, doctors, hospital and insurance company reps all gathered around a big table and televised on C-Span for the entire country to see. Transparency.

Apparently Democrat Senate Majority Leader Harry Reid of Nevada, Democrat House Speaker Nancy Pelosi of California, Democrat Senators Max Baucus of Montana, Christopher Dodd of Connecticut, and White House Chief of Staff Rahm Emanuel didn't see that speech. Either that or Barack Obama's words mean nothing. *(Fast forwarding to 2014: his words mean nothing.)*

Those individuals, sans any Republicans, Independents, doctors, nurses, insurance execs etc. are meeting behind closed doors, not on C-Span, to decide what 1/6 of the nation's total economy and 300,000,000 Americans health provider system will look like for generations to come. I'd be fearful of buying a used car from that bunch let alone trust them to destroy our current health care system and replace it with one that looks like it will offer 'less to more, cost trillions we don't have and still leave millions of Americans uninsured'. This power grab is called progress? Only in Washington, D.C.

What ever happened to the "transparency" we heard so much about during the campaign? Or did I miss all of those committee meetings, etc, that wee to be broadcast n C-Span? So far transparency seems to be missing in the Obama Administration; the administration that was purportedly based on "Change, change you can believe in." So much for words, which candidate Obama said many times, have meaning. Really?

When the politicians listed above complete their work, a Joint Conference Committee; mostly Democrats behind closed doors, before being voted on by both Houses, their product will be revised. Again, no televised C-Span hearings as Obama promised, definitely no "transparency." Duped again. We are so gullible.

Thanks for your time, Jaq

Thursday, October 22, 2009
Two Examples of Deceit...
by J. Wright

In my construction supervision days, there was a time when the boss had my Project Manager and me generate separate estimates of a major renovation of an existing home in the exclusive Rancho Santa Fe community north of San Diego.

It took us a couple of days and when we were finished, both of us, without conferring with the other, had an estimated cost of slightly more than $700,000.

With our estimates in hand, we ventured into the boss' office where he perused our numbers and began to redline out various portions. We asked, "Are those items being deleted from the project?"

"No," he answered, "Your numbers are too high."   *GASP!*

When the Senate Majority leader in Washington, D.C. attempted to remove about $250 billion dollars of future Medicare payments to doctors from the total cost of the proposed healthcare plan and pay for it "off budget" (*Read: add it to the annual deficit.*) the first thing I thought of was what my former employer attempted to create: a nice looking price, (*a "low-ball"*) but in the end, the home owner had to face the real cost of more than $700,000 as we had originally estimated.

I don't know what most folks would call a stunt like that, but the word *deceitful* comes to my mind. The same applies to what the Democrat Senate Majority Leader Harry Reid attempted. And to the credit of twelve Senators from his own party plus the opposing Republicans, his attempt failed miserably. Maybe that's a harbinger of things to come if and when a nationalized healthcare bill comes up for a vote.

No doubt our current health provider system needs improving. Beginning with a simpler plan we can afford financially seems more in order than to venture into the unknown and create additional unacceptable debt.

One such idea comes from the Coalition to Protect Patients' Rights, an organization that opposes congressional efforts to revamp the health-care system, the group opposes all the legislation being proposed in the House and Senate disallowing patients control of their healthcare.

The coalition's stance includes:
1. allowing people to buy insurance across state lines,
2. advocating for health savings accounts,
3. opposing the public option of government-run insurance and
4. giving patients vouchers and tax credits to purchase insurance.

The group also wants a revamping of medical malpractice suit filings *(Institute Tort Reform, in Washington-speak)*. Suit filings that they say adds billions to health-care costs annually. Quoting one of the doctors involved, "What we want is a system where the patient controls their own destiny."

Baby steps ... not a total overhaul of our existing system.

Thanks for your time, Jaq

Thursday, November 5, 2009

Socialized Health-Care Is Already on the Books

by J. Wright

In a televised interview recently, Dr. David Janda, orthopedic surgeon, University of Michigan, was featured as a guest. Janda, an author as well, is not a supporter of Obamacare in any fashion.

In his interview, he indicated that half of the proposed government take-over of our healthcare system is already law, "slipped" into the previous Stimulus package (H.R. 1 EH, The American Investment and Recovery Act of 2009) and will soon take effect. You remember that bill: $787 billion in borrowed dollars, more than 1,000 pages mostly unread.

Find it on the Internet at: *http://readthestimulus.org/hr1_final.txt*

Tragically, Dr. Janda indicated, no one from either party objected to the health provisions "slipped in" without discussion, which affects every one of us *(see pages 445, 454, 479)*. Our medical treatments will be tracked electronically by a new federal system. A new bureaucracy, the National Coordinator of Health Information Technology, will monitor treatments to make sure our doctors are doing what the federal government *(unelected bureaucrats)* deem appropriate and cost effective *(Read: allow)*. The goal is to have the remaining doctors, who haven't left the profession, forego autonomy and learn to operate less like solo practitioners. Hospitals and doctors that are not "meaningful users" of the new system will face severe penalties.

He also implied that if Obamacare passes into law, that 45% of the nation's current physicians will "retire" from practice. Add that fact to another, that more than 30 million newly insured will be expecting treatment and we will have a total mess.

The previous "Stimulus" bill, now law, generated yet another bureaucracy, the Federal Coordinating Council for Comparative Effectiveness Research *(see pages 190-192)*. Its goal is to slow the development and use of new medications and technologies because they allegedly drive up costs. Mercy! Talk about accepting the lowest common denominator!

Unfortunately, the elderly will be the hardest hit. As Democrat Tom Daschle wrote in his recent book, *"Seniors should be more accepting of the conditions that come with age instead of treating them."*

Keep in mind this is already the law of the land. "I'm from the government, I'm here to help." Doesn't make a lot of sense, does it?

Thanks for your time, Jaq

Wednesday, November 11, 2009

President Obama says Healthcare Overhaul Isn't About Him

(Really? So why is it called 'Obamacare'?)

by J. Wright

In August of this year, according to Senator Charles Grassley, (R-IA), *"A Democrat congressman last week told (him) after a conversation with the president that the president had trouble in the House of Representatives, and it wasn't going to pass if there weren't some changes made and the president says, "You're going to destroy my presidency."*

That president is none other than Barack H. Obama. The very same who stood in front of his vaunted teleprompter and asserted at various times that, *"...this (healthcare reform) isn't about me."*

The same *"destroy my presidency"* line was reportedly used as leverage on some of the reluctant Democrat Representatives in the House last week when President Obama caucused with them pushing for passage of Speaker Pelosi's 2,000+ page bill.

If it isn't about Obama, who is it about? It isn't about the majority of the taxpayers who will have to eventually pay for this boondoggle called reform. Since when does the legacy of a president take precedence over the welfare of the 307 million Americans to whom he swore an oath?

Poll after poll taken in recent weeks have shown a majority of Americans are not in favor of a government takeover of our current health provider system. Yes, changes must be implemented but not at the expense of destroying what is good about we have now.

Speaker Pelosi stood on the steps of the nation's capital and pronounced, *"...we have listened to the people."* Are these the same 'people' she insulted and derided as "un-Patriotic" following the Tea Party protests and Town Hall meetings last summer?

In my opinion, we have a self-serving, arrogant, out-of-control administration and legislative branch where tone-deaf elected officials totally ignore the wishes of their employers, the taxpayers. This is not the America where I grew up.

Thanks for your time, Jaq

November 13, 2009

<u>EDITOR: Viewpoint/Speak Out</u>

by J. Wright

A recent Cadillac News 'Speak Out' contributor says he is "flummoxed" by my opinions on the Health Care takeover. Join the crowd. In explanation, I'm flummoxed by the actions of our lawmakers in Washington who continue to ignore their constituents. Instead, they arrogantly forge ahead, readying to pass a bad bill rather than none at all.

The legislation recently passed by the Pelosi controlled House of Representatives, and the related bill considered in the Harry Reid Senate, are filled with massive tax hikes on individuals and small businesses. They enlarge existing federal bureaucracies, or create new ones empowered with overseeing family health care decisions, or deciding those personal decisions.

Remembering President Obama's oft repeated claim that "if you like your current insurance plan, you can keep it," it is estimated that current "reform" proposals in Congress would force between 90 million and 114 million Americans off their current insurance plans and into a government-approved, or government-run plan, if the "Public Option" is included.

Independent projections estimate the cost of these plans for a government takeover of health care will fall between $1 trillion and $2 trillion over the next decade; spending future tax dollars when the federal deficit today is at an all-time high and the national debt is skyrocketing. This while the nation is mired in a recession.

President Obama stresses that reform must lower, or "bend the curve" on rising health care costs. The 1,990 page bill passed in the Nancy Pelosi run House, or a larger one being considered by Harry Reid in the Senate, will do just the opposite; exponentially raising medical costs in this country while dramatically reducing quality of care. Inexplicably, millions of Americans will remain uninsured. What is the point, other than a massive power grab?

Reform? Higher taxes, increased costs and reduced quality of care in the guise of "reform" is not the "Change" American people expected. Will someone suggest to our elected representatives to "do no harm?"

Thanks for your time, Jaq

Thursday, November 19, 2009

Is Passing A Bad Bill Better Than Not Passing Any?

by J. Wright

Democrat Senate Majority Leader Harry Reid and Company, behind closed doors again, NOT in the glare of those C-Span cameras for all the world to see *(as Candidate Obama promised)* finally introduced the Senate's version of nationalized healthcare/insurance overhaul that the CBO estimates will cost $849 billion for the first ten years.

Of course the new taxes to pay for this boon-doggle begin now. The benefits, or lack of same, of the new plan will go into effect for the taxpayers six or seven years down the road, AFTER the 2012 elections. After the first ten years, who knows what the cost will be, or if the country will be solvent enough to afford it?

We've seen what happened to Medicare in the 25 years it has been in effect. It has exploded to ten times the cost of what was predicted by our "experts" in Washington. If "comprehensive healthcare reform" follows suit, our economy could totally collapse. There are areas where the government should not involve itself *(meddle)* and IMO, this is one of them. Besides, its constitutionality is questionable, but who is examining at that?

The nearly $250 billion *(1/4 trillion)* "Doctor fix," a stand-alone bill that strips a formula that automatically cuts Medicare physician payments out of "comprehensive" health reform, is still off budget, not paid for and raising the deficit. The Wall Street Journal writes, "This doctor maneuver is such a cleverly dishonest solution to their many contradictory promises that we're surprised Democrats didn't think of it sooner." Will President Obama look the other way and break another huge campaign promise and sign healthcare reform into law while knowing it will definitely increase the deficit?

It should be interesting to see how he reacts after being taken "to the wood shed" by the Red-Chinese over the ever expanding U.S. deficit, the incessant federal spending, and the threat of massive inflation in the future, which would place the billions of dollars the Red-Chinese have 'invested' in the U.S. government in jeopardy. The inmates are running the asylum and the Red-Chinese recognize that. Too bad the complicit MSM doesn't. They are too busy chasing former Governor Sarah Palin's skirt doing fact checks on her recent best-selling book. Too bad someone from the Fourth Estate didn't do as thorough a fact check on candidate Obama before the 2008 elections.

Thanks for your time, Jaq

Monday, November 23, 2009

"The High Costs of Dying..."

by J. Wright

Last Sunday I watched a portion of <u>60 Minutes</u> on CBS-TV. Their
first segment had to do with national healthcare. It began with an
opening statistic *(whose validity some might question)* claiming we
spend $50 billion annually in order to keep ailing seniors alive for an
additional two months or so in their last days. Is the "do no harm"
axiom now dependent on costs? Or on the sanctity of life?

We all should remember, it's still the PATIENT'S choice to linger in
possible pain with the HOPE *(Remember that word? A favorite of
many liberals)* that their condition might improve. Remember
another liberal favorite; CHOICE? It's not up to the Doctor or the
Government to decide. Not yet anyway

CBS, as self-appointed experts in medicine, national economics, and
most everything else under the sun, logically concluded in the case
of extending a fellow human's life for an indeterminate length of
time, that $50 billion dollars is obviously too much American capital
to waste. We need to become more "cost effective." Now they're
accountants too?

On October 19, Senate Democrat Majority Harry Reid stated almost
sneeringly that Medical Tort Reform would save "only" $50 billion a
year.

On August 31, 2009, the <u>NY Times</u> said medical tort reform is
moving to the fore of the healthcare debate, that medical malpractice
costs the system $50 billion a year. Oddly, the same Harry Reid
referred to that $50 billion as a *small fraction* of the $2 trillion that
healthcare reform would cost. Obviously a *faux pas* on Harry's part,
one of those nasty unintended consequences of forgetting which lie
to rely upon. His Senate bill claims to cost "only" $847 billion
during the next ten years. Do the math... multiply $50 billion ten

times: $500 billion? A small fraction, Harry?

If Medical Tort Reform were in place, how many fewer needless tests and costly medications would our current system push in order to prevent frivolous lawsuits? No, apparently it's easier to expect ailing seniors to just die rather than to take potential income away from fat trial lawyers, cronies who contribute tons of money to the Democrat Party. Sleaze politics at its best.

Is $50 Billion too much to spend on aging seniors or is it too little to save on overall healthcare? Decisions, decisions. It's still $50 billion every year. The Republican minority have insisted that any Healthcare Reform include ways to save billions in Tort Reform.

Democrat Majority Leader Harry Reid says no way. The Republicans also offered up eleven (11) amendments during the debate of these many bills, amendments that would force the lawmakers to drop what they have now and be insured like the rest of the country will be under their great plan. All eleven were nixed. These jokers are OUR employees, but who'd have guessed that?

$50 billion is either a drop in the bucket or it's a needless waste of money. It depends on where your values lie. My question is simple, why should appointed U.S. government bureaucrats now get into the business of determining when the ailing should die, or live, and for how long?

Proponents of the government plan say that "many" doctors feel that those final stabs at prolonging an uncomfortable life do more harm than good, and not much good. I say it doesn't matter what the doctors or the government "feels" or concludes. If the patient is awake, lucid and can communicate their wishes to either pull the plug or give it another try, it's their CHOICE.

How much longer we'll have the FREEDOM of CHOICE is debatable under this president and our current lawmakers. The lawmakers passed Medicare and Medicaid years ago to afford seniors some type of medical care... as usual; their numbers were way off the target, like ten times less than the actual costs when it panned out.

Quite a mistake. Now the Democrat lawmakers, seeing that mistake, want to take away between $450 - $500 billion in payments to doctors and care providers, who subsequently will NOT accept Medicare patients, or will discover a way to cut their losses like rationing care. *(Rationing? Death panels?)* Eventually, the elderly will be the ones left holding the bag.

This new healthcare boondoggle will cause thousands of doctors to retire or move off shore; it will add millions of people that are now uninsured and still leave millions of Americans without coverage. Care and treatment will not improve, costs will increase. The deficit will expand. Our debts to foreign nations will increase as well. It will ultimately insure illegal aliens *(for their future votes following amnesty legislation)* and worst, it will use taxpayer money to fund voluntary abortions. Those are the bad things. It's possible the good things that are included in the bill won't justify the bad.

What in hell are those lawmakers *(Democrats)* thinking? They seem all too willing to pass a really bad law instead of trying to improve the healthcare system we have now.

Thanks for your time, Jaq

Wednesday, December 16, 2009

Again, Pass Anything to Save Face
by J. Wright

Syndicated journalist Jennifer Rubin, in a commentary.com article, explains that the Democrats in the U.S. Senate are now at their wits end. Under mounting pressure, they have dropped "another hare-brained Harry Reid scheme." But what's next? The "ReidCare" public option idea has imploded along with adding more bodies to a failing Medicare including many who have reached 55 years of age. Ms. Rubin goes on, "They need, because a few centrists insist on it, something that is semi-coherent and that actually might allow the Democrats to face the voters, who currently disfavor ObamaCare by a huge margin. What's left after they take out the public option and the Medicare buy-in?"

A Republican leadership aide says, "What's left? $500 billion in Medicare cuts, $400 billion in tax increases, rising premiums, rising costs, thousands of onerous regulations, individual mandates, employer mandates, and expensive subsidies." So what's not to like? Seriously, just about everything, boys and girls. And this is reform?

A Democrat leadership aide explained it another way, similar to a Willy Sutton bank robbery gone badly. They're inside the bank surrounded outside by dozens of armed lawmen, their robbery plans went awry big time; they can leave the money and run, or shoot it out and take the money.

Apparently, it has come down to this in the Senate -- pass anything to save face and maybe give President Obama a boost in his plummeting job approval numbers, all at the expense of 1/6 of our faltering economy. Or maybe they can all go home, face their constituents and maybe clear their heads. When they return, maybe they can come up with a few inexpensive, discrete reforms that will have bipartisan support and not destroy our present system. Maybe? Pffft! When pigs fly.

Unfortunately, I see the Democrats, with their huge majority, as more than willing to pass anything just to pass it, *(...rather how Senator Bob Dole used to think)* regardless of the unintended consequences.

What we are witnessing in the Senate now are a few Dems and Harry Reid clustered behind closed doors again, not on C-Span as Obama the transparency candidate espoused, *(Remember?)* but working on a 'new' bill while the rest of the Senate is wasting time debating much of the old one.

Whatever passes the Senate, if it does, will then go to a Joint Conference Meeting with the Democrat Leaders of the Pelosi led House and who knows what will come from that? All of the recent talk about dropping the public option and the Medicare buy-in may suddenly be back in play, including abortion funding. And at what financial cost?

The problem is after it leaves the Joint Conference Committee, it takes only 51 votes in the Senate to pass it. Look for a few Democrat Senators, who may be in jeopardy in the upcoming 2010 elections, to seek political refuge and vote against it. Call it CYA, that's all it is.

Another problem, and a major problem at that, is that if this monstrosity is enacted it will be nearly impossible to rescind whilst Obama holds a veto pen, at least until the 2012 elections. If he is reelected in 2012 then we're really doomed. The America where many of us grew up will cease to exist.

Thanks for your time, Jaq

Wednesday, December 23, 2009

"What I Really Think of Healthcare Reform"
by J. Wright

My oldest daughter wrote to me recently asking my opinion of the proposed healthcare bill. This was my answer.

··· ··· ···

IF it were real healthcare reform, the end result would cover people that really can't afford insurance, yet many will still be uninsured; overall drug and treatment costs would decrease; physicians would not have to pay exorbitant malpractice insurance premiums; people could buy their insurance coverage anywhere they wished, they can't now; they would get income tax breaks for setting up a personal medical savings accounts. It seems that none of those things will take place.

Originally, they told us that 47 million Americans were without health insurance coverage. Then in a speech, President Obama lowered that number to 30 million. Now the experts are saying that after the passage of this bill, between 12 million and 30 million Americans will still NOT be insured. If that's the case, why are we bankrupting the country in the name of nationalized healthcare reform? What's the point? Power?

It's reform all right; it just doesn't do anything to improve on the health provider system we have now. Instead, it will succeed in indebting you and your future grandkids' grandkids for the rest of their lives with another wonderful expanding government entitlement program. All this is going to be done with borrowed or printed dollars; you do know that the federal government operates on the Fed's printed paper money, taxes and foreign loans don't you?

The government doesn't have any money of its own. It's not Obama's "stash" as some would believe.

Many current physicians have decided to retire early or leave the country when this is passed, and government estimates say that 30,000,000 additional people *(which doesn't add up)* will be added to the insurance roles. That means fewer doctors treating more people equals less than adequate medical care. That's something to look forward to.

Obama says this bill will create jobs: right, at the federal level. One report I read said that 118 new federal agencies *(bureaucracies)* will be needed to run this debacle. Who pays their salary? Yup, the U.S. taxpayer. Like we need a bigger, growing government.

Obama says this bill will lower the deficit. Not if you include the $240+ billion that is "off budget" in a separate bill called the "Doctor Fix." This is Medicare dollars that will be paid for services and for some reason, mostly to hoodwink the voters, is not included in this healthcare reform bill.

Then there's this pipe dream that Congress is going to "cut" $500 billion out of Medicare funding. When pigs fly, my dear. This $500 billion is a big part of the great savings and deficit reduction expectations that Obama and the Democrat lawmakers are crowing about. No Congress in our lifetime is ever going to "cut" Medicare funding. You can take that to the bank.

Taxes will increase on about everything now to pay for this thing so you wage earners, if you are still employed, will have less money for food, clothing, mortgages, utility bills and my grandkids' education. Forget anything else.

Most outrageous, the lawmakers we elected think they can force Americans to buy something, even if they don't want it. And if they don't buy it, they can be fined. And if they don't pay the fine, they can be penalized thousands of additional dollars and jailed.

Welcome to the USSA.

I've read the Constitution and can't seem to find where that's mentioned. There's also some mention of "equal protection under the law" in the Constitution. Some states are receiving preferential treatment in order to garner needed Senate votes in order to pass this monstrosity. Time will tell if any court in the land has the will to stand up and declare this mess illegal.

Does that answer your question, dear?

Love, Dad~

··· ··· ···

Thanks for your time, Jaq

Thursday, December 31, 2009
<u>Connect the Dots? What Dots?</u>
by J. Wright

Apparently, before socialist leaning Democrat supporters begin to ravenously "eat their own'" they must start nibbling around the edges as noted New York Times columnist, Maureen Dowd, did in a surprising column published recently. For sure, Ms. Dowd dutifully injected her customary "Bush Derangement Syndrome" attacks, including attacks on former VP Cheney and Secretary of Defense Rumsfeld, but by no means did she show any pity for President Obama and his pitiful national security team's recent actions.

I wish she had gone farther. What are we watching today in our intelligence gathering circles? The same type of "'intelligence wall" that stifled two previous administrations with political infighting?

Have we forgotten the "Jamie Gorelick Wall" that was in vogue under President Clinton barring anti-terror investigators from accessing information or communicating with other federal security agencies? The "'Wall'" that the 9/11 Commission eliminated and later set up guidelines to be implemented that would improve our future security?

It's deja vu all over again, or close to it. Instead of being able to connect the dots, the current Obama Administration security heads are seemingly unable to recognize a dot when it's handed to them, and the President is too busy vacationing or playing golf to bother with an immediate acknowledgement of a near miss above our own soil. *(Circa Detroit, MI: the 'Underwear Bomber'.)*

Instead we got unbelievable spin *(blather)* from Janet Napolitano, the current Secretary of Homeland Security about how well "the system" worked. 'The system' was an alert passenger on the plane, upon seeing what the would be bomber was up to, took him out, saving the passengers lives and the plane. 'System'? I laugh.

The next day she reversed herself and said she was misunderstood; taken out of context. Had those remarks been uttered by Tom Ridge or Michael Chertoff, a couple of President Bush's security chiefs, they would surely have been verbally tarred and feathered within hours by the national media and Democrat lawmakers and asked to submit their resignations post haste.

How's that "hope and change" working today? Not so hot as far as our national security is concerned, but Al Queda seems to be thriving under it. Unfortunately, until the 2012 elections we are stuck with this amateurish administrative 'Lost Gonzo' posse that President Obama has trotted out to lead our country

Happy New Year readers, good riddance to 2009!

Thanks for your time, Jaq

Monday, January 4, 2010

"Standing..." You Either Have It Or You Don't

by J. Wright

Every time I see the U.S. Supreme Court mentioned regarding the possible constitutionality of a new bill, that Congress in its infinite wisdom has just passed into law, my head wants to explode; reason being, I don't fully understand the legality of the term "'standing.'"

It's my understanding that in order to bring a case before the SC Justices, the plaintiff(s) or ones bringing suit, must have "standing,'" because apparently the Court is not allowed to simply open a case on their own because of public sentiment or pressure, or even if they might think in their own minds that a law, or portion of it, is unconstitutional.

If we examined all of the laws Congress has passed in the past decade or longer and examined them for constitutionality, I'd wager many of them wouldn't pass muster, but still they remain on the books. Why, because someone with "standing" didn't bother to make a federal case out of it? Or if someone did, a liberal federal judge in a lower court threw the case out before it reached the high court in Washington, D.C.

Or, trial lawyers being what they are and whom they support *(Read: the liberal left in our political family)* are not necessarily apt to take up such mundane matters as constitutionality. But I digress.

Definition of "standing" in part says, "...that in the United States, the current doctrine is that a person cannot bring a suit challenging the constitutionality of a law unless the plaintiff can demonstrate that the plaintiff is *(or will imminently be)* harmed by the law. Additionally, the party suing must have something to lose in order to sue unless they have automatic standing by action of law."

If Congress passes a law next week mandating that all Americans MUST buy health insurance or be fined, and if the individual doesn't pay that fine they will be penalized a much larger amount and jailed, isn't that "'having something to lose?'" Such as one's liberty? Or is our loss of liberty just a foregone conclusion nowadays? Maybe the key word up there is "imminently."

Imminently we may find out. Or not.

Thanks for your time, Jaq

Wednesday, January 6, 2010
Republicans May Use SCOTUS to Stop Healthcare Reform
by J. Wright

Imagine that, the Republicans using one of the liberal Democrats favorite secondary legislative bodies, the Courts, to stop healthcare reform in its tracks.

In a recent blog, I brought up the issue of "standing" as it applies to who can bring, or file a legal suit, with the United States Supreme Court. In order to bring a case before the Justices the plaintiff(s) or the ones suing, must have "'standing",' because apparently the Court is unable to open a case on their own, even if they suspect that a law, or portion of it, is unconstitutional.

By definition in part, "standing" means, "...that in the United States, the current doctrine is that a person cannot bring a suit challenging the constitutionality of a law unless the plaintiff can demonstrate that the plaintiff is *(or will imminently be)* harmed by the law.

Additionally, the party suing must have 'something to lose' in order to sue unless they have automatic standing by action of law."

Retired Judge Andrew Napolitano, FOX Cable News analyst, recently confirmed that definition. Any citizen of the United States that will be harmed by the law, in this case, forced to buy health insurance under threat of financial fine or possible imprisonment, can bring suit because they have "standing."

Judge Napolitano went on to say that if the pending healthcare reform legislation that is now being negotiated behind closed doors, not on C-Span as promised by Candidate Obama several times, is passed into law, a private citizen can seek relief and have the law deemed unconstitutional. Napolitano added that such action could also open the doors to looking at various other laws whose constitutionality has been questioned.

At this moment, Senator Orin Hatch, R-Utah, is putting this issue in motion. He can't bring the suit personally but surely he will find an American citizen willing and able to do so. Time will tell.

Hatch and other Senators are arguing that the bill's requirement *(the Individual Mandate)* that most people buy insurance or face a penalty violates the Constitution's ban on taking private property for public purpose without just compensation.

Also, that a provision that could treat some insurance companies in Louisiana, Nebraska and Michigan different from others is a violation of the 14th Amendment's "equal protection" clause.

The AG from Texas just joined in claiming that Congress can't force citizens to buy anything, including health insurance, by saying it falls under the Interstate Commerce clause. Now it's getting serious, boy and girls.

The Attorneys General are using the "law of the land," our Constitution and the protections it affords the citizenry, to take a hard look at this mess the Democrats call reform.

Thanks for your time, Jaq…

Tuesday, January 12, 2010

Healthcare Reform? Great for Some; Crappy for Others!

by J. Wright

Quoting a CBS News poll in part, "President Obama's approval rating on handling healthcare is at an all-time low. Just 36 percent of Americans approve of Mr. Obama's handling of healthcare, according to the poll, conducted from Jan. 6 – 10. Fifty-four percent disapprove."

The Wall Street Journal opined last October, "…it may well be the worst piece of post-New Deal legislation ever introduced." Since then it has worsened. There is little voter consensus that the reforms under consideration represent the right approach. Only about one in five Americans thinks the reforms strike the right balance when it comes to expanding coverage, controlling costs and regulating insurance companies. Worse, congressional experts say 15 to 30 million Americans will still be left uninsured. Again I ask, what's the point?

Now the Democrats and some of their special interest supporters are again bickering about a thing labeled "Cadillac Insurance" policies, or blanket coverage that is the very best an individual can possibly enjoy in today's market. The final bill now being considered would assess a huge tax on the value of those policies. Some special interest groups, financial supporters of Democrat lawmakers, are now discovering that they were not exempted, especially many of the millions of labor union members. They are furious and are making their displeasure known at some of the "Sweetheart" favoritism deals handed out by Democrat Senate Majority Leader Harry Reid at the expense of everyone else.

Curious, why should a law grant some Americans special treatment and force others to pay higher costs? Constitutional scholars in opposition cite the 14th amendment guaranteeing "equal protection under the law." In real reform, wouldn't all Americans at the least be provided with improved healthcare coverage including lowered costs? This bill is allowing "better than equal protection" for a few several special interest groups. How constitutional is that?

Thanks for your time, Jaq

Wednesday, January 20, 2010
<u>Why is it Impossible for Democrats to Learn from History?</u>
by J. Wright

If you recently recovered from a coma, or haven't been paying attention to the national political scene of late, the commonwealth of Massachusetts just held a special election to permanently fill the seat in the United States Senate left open with the recent passing of liberal Democrat Senator Edward *(Ted)* Kennedy. Against all odds and contrary to history, the voters in Massachusetts elected a conservative Republican to fill that seat.

This from <u>The Globe</u> Newspapers: "Voter anxiety and resentment, building for months in a troubled economy, exploded like a match on dry kindling in the final days of the special election for US Senate.

In arguably the most liberal state in the nation, a Republican - and a conservative one at that - won and will crash the Bay State's all-Democratic delegation with a mandate to kill the healthcare overhaul pending in Congress."

Yes, it appears that the outcome of this special election has ramifications as far away as Washington, D.C. where several Democrat lawmakers who narrowly won elections in 2008 are having second thoughts about their future employment if they continue to blindly follow Obama/Reid/Pelosi off the cliff in support of this thing being hashed over behind closed doors called "healthcare reform."

The president and his Democrat legislative leaders have been unsuccessful in passing an extremely unpopular deficit-busting bill for the past year while the national economy has sputtered and unemployment has climbed to near record levels. Because the Democrats couldn't agree amongst themselves they decided their cover is to blame their failures on the Republicans, who weren't invited to participate in the first place. Even the loss of the Democrat Senatorial hopeful in Massachusetts has been blamed on past Republican policies. They can't be serious. Question: did they learn anything from this loss?

Thanks for your time, Jaq

Wednesday, February 3, 2010

Rhetoric Galore: No Action

by J. Wright

In political forums other than Blogspot.com, I have suggested that it's more important to watch what President Obama does rather than listening and taking what he says 'to the bank.' Much of the time they are at odds, and for one, I find that difficult to accept in anyone. As another writer posted recently, *"Platitudes about America and the American people which, when he says them, simply do not ring true. They are words being mouthed but not believed by him."*

Borrowing a paragraph from a blog recently submitted here at: Top of the Ticket, by Andrew Malcolm on 1/29/2010: *"A startling new poll just out: It shows that fully 9 out of 10 Americans bought that State of the Union gimmick of President Obama's to impose an alleged spending freeze on parts of the federal budget to carve into the nation's deficit that's expanding faster than a billion bellies at Super Bowl snack time."*

May I add, this is one person that didn't buy into it, and here's why: In the past year, President Obama's budget increased federal spending by somewhere near 20% … an amazing increase compared to former budgets. Now, supposedly switching to a more populist, or man-on-the-street, pro little-guy approach, he's now proposing a "freeze" on federal spending. To me, this is akin to locking the barn door after the horse is gone.

Noted columnist Charles Krauthammer, said on FOX Cable News recently: *"It is not a hatchet or scalpel, it is a Q-tip, it is a fraud. This is a miniscule amount. It excludes defense, homeland security. It excludes Veterans Affairs. It excludes all the entitlements, which are 60% of the budget. It excludes stimuli past and future. The two-thirds of the new $1 trillion stimulus that has not been spent. All of that is excluded. It excludes the trillion that would end up being spent in healthcare, if it were passed. What it is, is a $15 billion reduction in a year, 2011, in which the CBO has just announced we're going to have a deficit of $1.35 trillion. It's a rounding error. It's lunch money."*

Scratching away the nine zeroes in billions and creating a fraction using the $1.35 trillion weighed against the $15 billion in so-called reductions gives one a fraction that looks like 15/1,350, or farther, 1/90 which is equal to 0.011% if you prefer percentages. As Dr. Krauthammer said: *'A Q-tip, a fraud.'* Or as I am deign to say, *'Same ol' crap, different flies.'*

$15 billion… *($15,000,000,000.00)* a big savings in Obama's eyes and in the eyes of 9 out of 10 of those polled. Democrat Senate Majority Leader Harry Reid, in discussing one of the Senate Republicans failed health reform amendments, sneered at a "mere" $50 billion in annual savings if real medical tort reform were implemented thereby creating a much needed savings on health providers malpractice insurance premiums.

Fancy. I guess it depends on whose billions we are talking about. Actually, all of those billions are either taxpayer's dollars or dollars borrowed abroad from foreign interests. The government has no money of its own but our elected lawmakers and President Obama seem to have forgotten that minor detail.

Thanks for your time, Jaq

Tuesday, February 16, 2010
Ideologues or Just Slightly to the Left?
by J. Wright

President Obama met with some Republican Congressional leaders recently and asserted, "I'm not an ideologue. I'm not." Oddly enough that statement took me back to November of 1973 when President Nixon uttered the memorable words, "I'm not a crook." Many of us recall how that ended the following summer.

Whether President Obama is an ideologue or not is up for grabs, it's not for me to decide. I do however look at those with whom one associates as one measure of a person's core beliefs. Take some of his more controversial Czar appointments, high level, executive posts not confirmed by Congress and with little to no Congressional oversight.

Former Green Jobs Czar Van Jones for example, now resigned, an admitted Communist whom presidential aide Valerie Jarret once said, "We've had out eyes on him for a long time." That's comforting.

Then there's the Guantanamo Closure Czar Daniel Fried who believes that the U.S. caused the war on terrorism and that terrorists should be granted legal rights above those of our citizenry.

John Brennan, Obama's Terrorism Czar, has had a ton of face time on TV recently in attempting to explain the Christmas 'Underwear' Bombing suspect folly. Brennan has no diplomatic or governmental affairs experience, supports open borders and the disbandment of the U.S. Military. Beyond that, he is anti-CIA. Swell.

Weapons Czar Aston Carter wants all weapons in the U.S. destroyed and the U.N. gun ban on all firearms put in place.

Obama's WMD Czar Gary Samore seeks to destroy all WMD beginning with the U.S. arsenal first, a unilateral move as a "show of good faith." Did I mention that he is a former Communist too? Of some thirty or more Czars, these are just a few of the extremist folks appointed in recent months to oversee our nation's future. Ideologues? You decide.

Thanks for your time, Jaq

Thursday, March 11, 2010
To Fish, or Not to Fish? That's the Rub
by J. Wright

Robert Montgomery of ESPN Outdoors.com wrote recently that the Obama administration will accept no more public input for a federal strategy that could prohibit U.S. citizens from fishing the nation's oceans, coastal areas, Great Lakes, and even inland waters. He goes on to say, "Now we see NOAA (National Oceanic and Atmospheric Administration) and the Obama administration planning the future of recreational fishing access in America based on a similar agenda of these same groups and other Big Green anti-use organizations, through an Executive Order by the President."

Conversely, Deadbeat.com says that ESPN's anti-recreational fishing allegation is false; a rumor. I'm not familiar with Deadbeat.com but they are linked to an extremely liberal Mediamatters.com and that raises some skepticism on my part. AP and several other Internet news sources have published this report so I guess it's up to you the readers to choose what to believe.

In a nutshell however, President Obama, in order to assuage the Green Environmentalist special interest lobby, could with one stroke of a pen with an Executive Order make it illegal for you to take your boat out on Lakes Cadillac or Mitchell here in my northern Michigan neighborhood and attempt to catch a fish for dinner. If that becomes the case, welcome to the new, fundamentally changed, USSA.

Where does the federal government get the authority to decide what takes place on an isolated body of water? According to political author, James Brovard, when Obama's current Climate Czar Carol Browner headed up the EPA under President Clinton in the 1990s, she implemented what was referred to as the "Glancing Goose Test". Geese being migratory birds, fly across state borders. The theory is that if they glance down and see a body of water, no matter its size, then as migratory border crossing birds, any water they see falls under the auspices of the Interstate Commerce clause. Is that a stretch?

This "test" was thrown out of court once but the Browner EPA ignored the ruling. Apparently, the Obama administration may be ignoring it today, or they're not. Time will certainly tell.

Good fishing before all of this comes to pass. I can't begin to imagine the public outcry if indeed it does.

Thanks for your time, Jaq

Saturday, May 8, 2010
<u>Social Justice? I have a couple of questions.</u>

Seven Principles of Social Justice:

1. Every citizen willing to work shall receive a just and living annual wage, which will enable him to maintain and educate his family.

2. Nationalize those public necessities, which by their very nature are too important to be held in the control of private individuals.

3. Uphold the right of private property yet of controlling it for the public good.

4. Believe not only in the right of the laboring man to organize in unions but also in the duty of the Government which that laboring man supports to protect these organizations against the vested interests of wealth and of intellect.

5. Believe in the event of a war and for the defense of our nation and its liberties, if there shall be a conscription of men let there be a conscription of wealth.

6. Believe in preferring the sanctity of human rights to the sanctity of property rights.

7. Believe that the chief concern of government shall be for the poor, because as is witnessed, the rich have ample means of their own to care for themselves.

So, boys and girls, does any of that sound vaguely familiar?

Q- *Who proposed it and when?*
Well, as today's progressive liberal socialist types are suggesting, it wasn't Glenn Beck, who is now being compared to Father Coughlin, the Canadian priest and radical leftist from FDR's era.

This crap was proposed in November of 1934. Father Coughlin, who migrated to American in the early 1930s, became a nationally known voice on the radio with upwards of 25 million listeners.

Originally an avid foe of FDR and his policies, *because FDR wasn't liberal enough,* he sucked up to him anyway in hopes of becoming Secretary of the Treasury. This from a man who was both anti-capitalism and anti-commerce. Whoa! Sounds a lot like what we are hearing today from some of our leaders.

After eighty years and more of this crap slowly taking over, spreading like a venomous cancer into our lives and our kids and grandkids lives, is it time to eradicate it? November 2 can't come soon enough.   Thanks for your time, Jaq~

May 8, 2010

EDITOR: Viewpoint/Speak Out

by J. Wright

As a rule, I don't become easily disturbed but that's beginning to change of late. When Attorney General Eric Holder and Secretary of Homeland Security Janet Napolitano criticized the Arizona anti-illegal immigration law *(emphasis on illegal)* then admit publicly that they haven't read it *(it's about 16 pages in length)* I begin to become disturbed.

That was nothing until President Obama invited the President of Mexico, Felipe Calderone, to the White House and where the next day Calderone stood in the "people's house," our House of Representatives, and parroting Obama, defamed Arizona's governor and legislature for passing the law, following which the majority of the Democrat legislators in attendance stood and applauded.

Outrageous!

Now John Morton, Obama's head of the U.S. Immigration and Customs Enforcement (ICE) said his agency would not necessarily process illegal immigrants referred to him by the state of Arizona. "The best way to reduce illegal immigration is with a comprehensive federal approach, not a patchwork of state laws," he said.

Echoing previous comments made by President Obama and others in the administration, Morton said that Arizona's new law targeting illegal immigration is not "good government. I don't think the Arizona law, or laws like it, are the solution."

The real irony in what President Obama believes and what AG Eric Holder, Secretary Napolitano and ICE head Morton said is that the *Arizona* law is redundant in that it mimics the existing but currently unenforced federal statute that makesit a crime (a misdemeanor) to be in a state illegally and requires law officials to check suspects for immigration paperwork

Someone please explain why our federal agencies refuse to enforce an existing statute? Maybe because the current administration sees those illegally amongst us as possible registered Democrats with voting rights one day?

Source: newsbusters.com and more than a dozen other Internet web sites.

Thanks for your time, Jaq

Sunday, May 16, 2010

EDITOR: <u>Political Dissent? Patriotic or anti-American?</u>

by J. Wright   *(A Letter of mine as published recently in the Cadillac News.)*

Seton Motley, writing in <u>dallasblog.com</u> says, "Supreme Court nominee Elena Kagan wrote in a 1996 article titled *Private Speech, Public Purpose: The Role of Governmental Motive in First Amendment Doctrine* that "redistribution of speech is not itself an illegitimate end" for government. Ms. Kagan also asserts that government can restrict speech if it believes that speech might cause harm, either directly or by inciting others to do harm."

Quoting Peg Kaplen on <u>typepad.com</u>, "Dissent is the Highest Form of Patriotism." So we were told just a few short years ago (even by Hillary Clinton: see below).

When we had a Republican president, those on the left constantly reminded us that speaking out against the government was our right, a higher calling - and that criticism of such was anti-American and wrong.

Remember When Dissent Was Patriotic? When doing it didn't mean you were a zealot or an extremist or a Nazi? Hillary Clinton once thought debate and dissent were patriotic. Or, at least, she did back in 2003 when she said, *"I am sick and tired of people who say that if you debate and you disagree with this (Bush) administration somehow you're not patriotic. We should stand up and say 'we are Americans and we have a right to debate and disagree with any administration'."*

I totally agreed with then Senator Clinton. But unless I'm mistaken, anymore it seems like this Freedom of Speech thingy, established by the Founders in our Constitution, depends wholly on who is speaking, or who is currently occupying the White House, or who controls the legislative branches of our government.

When Supreme Court nominee Kagan is confronted with her own words during the upcoming Senate Judiciary Committee hearings, what do you suppose her answers will reflect today? Will she, like President Obama, lament that "information becomes a distraction?"

Thanks for your time, Jaq

May 26, 2010

<u>EDITOR: Viewpoint/Speak Out</u>

by J. Wright

Representative Tom Price, Republican-GA, wrote in part recently:

Democrats in Congress are gearing up to vote on new legislation that blatantly undermines the First Amendment. Known as the DISCLOSE Act (HR 5175), responding to the recent Supreme Court ruling in *Citizens United v. Federal Election Commission.* The Court found that the federal government could not restrict the free speech rights of individuals or other entities wishing to participate in the political dialogue; a right under the Constitution's First Amendment, and which the Supreme Court upheld.

The White House and their allies on Capitol Hill now see honest criticism as a threat to their big government, liberal agenda.

Under this DISCLOSE Act, certain incorporated entities would be restricted in how they can exercise their free speech rights, but there is an exemption for some in the media sphere like newspapers, TV news, etc. However, there is one driving force in today's public debate that is NOT exempt; Internet bloggers *(of which I'm one).*

Representative Price adds, "…many bloggers, in order to exercise their free speech rights, would have to jump through the same onerous new hoops…" and he calls it an overreach by one party in power.

Representative Price ends his article with this: "Democrats should not be allowed to give themselves carte blanche to shut down the ability of those in the blogosphere or elsewhere to participate in our nation's collective dialogue. That flies in the face of our most sacred rights as American citizens."

As I wrote here recently, political dissent today is viewed by many radical leftists as unpatriotic. A few short years ago it was championed by many of the same politicians who are willing now to put "their boot on some necks." In other words, we should all sit down and shut up.

Source: *http://biggovernment.com/tprice/2010/05/27/bloggers-beware-theyre-coming-after-you/*

Thanks for your time, Jaq

Saturday, June 12, 2010

Feds Seek To Bail Out Faltering Newspapers

by J. Wright

Taken from the Washington Times.com, June 7, 2010:

"The Federal Trade Commission (FTC) is seeking ways to 'reinvent' journalism, and that's a cause for concern. According to a May 24 draft proposal, the agency thinks government should be at the center of a media overhaul. The bureaucracy sees it as a problem that the Internet has introduced a wealth of information options to consumers, forcing media companies to adapt and experiment to meet changing market needs. FTC's policy staff fears this new reality.

"There are reasons for concern that experimentation may not produce a robust and sustainable business model for commercial journalism," the report states. With no faith that the market will work things out for the better, government thinks it must come to the rescue.

Former President Ronald W. Reagan might say, "There they go again." IMO, this government is again attempting to dally in the business of micro-managing private businesses. They can barely govern at all yet they see fit to inject themselves into places where the public sector can and does function more efficiently. This latest proposal is about attempting to salvage struggling newsprint publications *(referred by some to as "dead tree" media)* that, in the eyes of the bureaucrats and politicians, "are too big to fail." Based on recent results, such actions always come at a price with political strings attached *(remember GM, Chrysler and the major banks?)*. How could any newsprint company perform objectively after receiving public taxpayer dollars and NOT seem to be under the boot heel of the government? Not that many aren't biased already.

Again, the camel sneaks its nose under the proverbial tent. Allow government an inch, you know the rest. The Times adds: "Fostering a robust public-policy debate, not saving a particular business model, should be the goal of journalism in the first place."

Thanks for your time, Jaq~

July 17, 2010

EDITOR: Viewpoint/Speak

by J. Wright

Tuesday, while driving home from downtown, I caught a snippet of a conservative radio talk show hosted by Roger Hedgecock, a popular San Diego based talk-show personality. He was talking to a caller who suggested that we *(the federal government)* need to reduce spending and suggested a method of starting out with a stated percentage each year across the board.

To the untrained political analyst that may have sounded like a great idea   *(If one could get past the federal bureaucracy heads.)*

Since Mr. Hedgecock *is* a trained political analyst, he explained why it never works. First, Congress floats a trial balloon stating that they are going make across the board cuts by say 5% … not huge. Then the various federal departments and agencies that are going to "suffer" those cuts go public.

Hedgecock suggested that the Department of Defense for example, instead of weeding out redundant departments and unnecessary programs and ridding itself of non-essential employees would instead advertise that they would not proceed with the building of another super carrier … which in Hedgecock's estimation would have Congressmen and constituents alike, that might benefit from the construction of that carrier, lining up to protest. Ergo the Defense budget remains the same or increases.

The Defense Department was just one example Hedgecock recited. He added that every federal agency or department, all run by federally appointed bureaucratic heads and civil service employees, would utilize the same public relations campaign, all in an effort to save their annual budgets and remain "in business." Change? Forget about it.

Several years ago, author James Brovard wrote several books describing a "shadow government" consisting of the various federal bureaucracies. Many Americans fail to realize their power; that they and the aforementioned unelected agency managers and civil servants cause most of the problems we face in this ever-expanding government.

Thanks for your time, Jaq~

July 28, 2010

EDITOR: Viewpoint/Speak Out

by J. Wright

Twice of late, I've written on the redundancy of federal agencies enacting various policies resulting in horrific spending. Spending that ultimately results in the waste of scarce taxpayer dollars and the inability to convince federal agency heads to, in all conscience, find ways to reduce waste and spending.

Here are a few four-year-old examples of known duplication and overlap in government programs: in 1996 there were 788 federal education programs in 40 agencies costing $100 billion annually; 117 federal programs aimed at at-risk youth in 15 agencies costing $4.4 billion; 342 economic development programs managed by 13 agencies with little coordination among them.

It goes on: the FDA and 11 other federal agencies administered over 35 different laws that oversee food safety; 17 different programs in 8 different federal agencies administer rural water and wastewater programs; over 90 early childhood education programs are in 11 federal agencies and 20 offices; 163 job training programs administered by 15 different federal agencies costing about $20 billion. Remember, this was four years ago: it's grown worse today.

None of the above touches on the spending of federal agencies involved in combating terrorism, or "the War on Drugs," or the then 20 different federal agencies or departments assessing the threat to U.S. national security from weapons of mass destruction.
Worse, recent programs passed under President Obama have increased the number of new federal agencies and the federal civil service employee payroll substantially, with no end in sight.

On the plus side, President Obama signed a bill this week toward eliminating unbelievable billions in "erroneous" payments made to approximately 20,000 dead people and 14,000 convicted felons. Still, the number of federal agencies and wasteful spending has to be reined in further. That or the nation eventually goes belly-up. Or, maybe that's the objective.

Source:
http://answers.yahoo.com/question/index;_ylt=Apzje4MA_.vrU5bq3 Fxp46AjzKIX;_ylv=3?qid=20100524215736AA9jCdB

Thanks for your time, Jaq

August 18, 2010

EDITOR: Viewpoint/Speak Out

by J. Wright

For decades, the University of Michigan Wolverine's biggest rival in Big Ten football has been the Ohio State University Buckeyes, now it seems we may have another inter-state rivalry brewing with Ohio: job creation.

John Kasich, Republican gubernatorial candidate in Ohio is running against incumbent Democrat Governor Ted Strickland and Kasich has a commanding 6-8 percentage point lead in recent polls.

Governor Strickland, similar to Michigan's Governor Jennifer Granholm, has not been able to pull his state out of the stagnant recession that has plagued most of the nation. John Kasich was Chairman of the House Appropriations Committee under then Speaker Newt Gingrich during the 104th through the 106th Congress from 1994 through 2000 when the nation enjoyed a budget surplus.

A Kasich win in Ohio could be a harbinger of bad things to come for either of Michigan's gubernatorial candidates: Democrat Virg Bernero, or Republican Rick Snyder, in that Kasich has the political smarts to possibly rescue Ohio from the morass of this stagnant economy. He did it when in Washington, I'm confident he can do it in Ohio.

Kasich has some sound ideas about bringing jobs back to foundering Ohio. If Michigan's new Governor has any workable ideas himself, it would be prudent to hit the bricks running so to speak and not allow neighboring Ohio to get out front. Of course, no Governor can do it all by themselves. In Michigan's case it will take some major cooperation between both Houses of the Legislature, something we have rarely seen around here.

My suggestion: vote on November 2, keep your eyes on the Ohio race, and then hope for the best here at home.

Thanks for your time, Jaq

September 21, 2010
EDITOR: Viewpoint/Speak Out
by J. Wright

I wrote recently that Ohio might do well fiscally to elect Republican John Kasich as governor. Kasich was a former Chairman of the United States House of Representatives Appropriations Committee in charge of allocating taxpayer dollars for federal projects and operational expenses. During Kasich's three terms as Chairman, the government ran a budgetary surplus. Kasich is basing his gubernatorial campaign on creating jobs for Ohioans.

Michigan's outgoing governor, Jennifer Granholm, just released her ideas for balancing Michigan's budget, which at last count, was about $920 million in the red. Nowhere did I see her mention any plans for new job creation though she must have some ideas along those lines.

Another neighbor of both Ohio and Michigan is Indiana, a smaller state both in size and population but unlike either, has a Republican Governor *and a budget surplus*, sometimes referred to as their "rainy day" fund. Earlier this year it amounted to about $1.3 billion. To make ends meet during these difficult times, their state officials cut $669 million in spending. Indiana lawmakers also reduced the state's reserves down to $830 million.

Little Indiana has $830 million in reserve and Michigan has a deficit of $930 million. It doesn't make sense. At the risk of sounding partisan, could having Republican Mitch Daniels as Governor have made a difference? There's an answer somewhere.

I applaud Jennifer Granholm for wanting to balance the budget, it is also a <u>requirement written into the State's constitution</u>. Like Ohio's John Kasich, it's my opinion that jobs are the catalyst to any fiscal solution. Jobs create taxes, from employees as well as their employers. Taxes run the state's economy.

With the November 2 elections about ten weeks away, I'd like to see Michigan's plans for job creation; not just unsubstantiated rhetoric claiming past saved or created jobs.

Sources:
http://sunshinereview.org/index.php/Indiana_state_budget &
http://www.michigan.gov/budget/0,1607,7-157-21329---F,00.html

Thanks for your time, Jaq

September 15, 2010
EDITOR: Viewpoint/Speak Out
by J. Wright

I came across an article by journalist Jonathan Alter where he writes, "Michigan Democrats are expressing concern about the political security of Rep. John D. Dingell, 84, who has been elected to the House a record 28 times since first winning office in a 1955 special election."

Alter added, "… this comes on the heels of Dingell ramping up his fundraising and warning donors that he needs their help to make sure he can define Steele *(supported by Tea Partiers)* and win a seat that only he and his father have held since 1933."

Fascinating … does anyone else see anything curious here? I don't know Representative John Dingell personally, but I have a problem with any elected official, regardless of who he is, holding office for 56 consecutive years. Add his father's terms to that and between the two, their terms reach beyond the time I have been on this planet.

I may be alone in this thinking but from my perspective, any politician in office for that long may be part of the problem we are experiencing in Washington, D.C. today.

I don't know the Republican candidate, Mr. Steele, either; the district he and Dingell are running in are far away from Cadillac, but, if he is being supported by the Tea Partiers, I personally don't see that as a disadvantage or a negative mark against him. From the results across the nation in last Tuesday's primary elections, many candidates that had Tea Party support won handily. There must be something in their principles that appeals to ordinary voters weary of the proposed taxation policies and massive federal spending programs that will continue to indebt our great-grandchildren and their grandchildren. Not to mention stifling a staggering, stagnant economy today.

Source:
http://www.politico.com/news/stories/0910/42191.html#ixzz0zeZqRK S5

Thanks for your time, Jaq~

September 27, 2010
EDITOR: Viewpoint/Speak Out
by J. Wright

Some of my friends, more like … some of my past liberal friends, who shun me because of my views and postings here, said I was being too critical of Mr. Obama, both as a candidate, now as our president. OK, I'll concede that, but this is an opinion forum and those were my opinions then. After his inauguration, I lightened up and for the past several months, I haven't written anything too critical of the man, other than commenting on some of his hare-brained policies. I won't now either. Today I saw this question and comment published on Heritage.com:

"Will the federal government continue to spend more, tax more, control more, and defend our liberties less? Or will we choose a new and bolder direction that returns power to the people? All indications are that we are approaching one of those pivotal moments in our political history, a tipping point. It will be a test of our national character."

President Obama, campaigning to keep Democrats in office, claims that electing Republicans will surely take the country back to the "failed policies of the former Bush administration." *(One of those "failed policies" that I distinctly recall was the joblessness rate hovered around 4.5%, compared to a whopping 9.5% today. Give me more of those "failed policies" please.)*

Besides the high unemployment rate, the Obama Administration policies have provided us with questionable, excessive spending, more taxes, less control over our individual lives, and less defense of our liberties. Not exactly the "Hope and Change" we were promised in 2008. Now, less than two years later, after we elected this liberal government, this is where we find ourselves. Is it Obama's fault? Probably not, no more than the claims that everything that went wrong previously were Bush's fault.

We elected the politicians that brought us to this place.
Source:http://blog.heritage.org/2010/09/27/morning-bell-the-heritage-pledge/

Thanks for your time, Jaq

December 9, 2010

<u>EDITOR: Viewpoint/Speak Out</u>

by J. Wright

Today, for my first time, I saw our current federal tax rates referred to in print as the "Bush Tax Rates, not the "Bush Tax Cuts." Strange why the main stream media and the liberal Democrats continually refer to them as "Tax Cuts," neither of them chose for years to call the marginal rates increased by President Clinton, as a result of vice-President Al Gore's tie breaking vote in the Senate, as the "Clinton Tax Hikes." Not exactly "fair and balanced" in my opinion.

We have a proposal in the pipelines now to re-institute the Estate Tax and at a rate of 35%. My 'estate' wouldn't qualify, I'm far too poor … but for those that do, it amounts to this; an individual works lifelong and accumulates an estate, all on the leftover dollars that the feds, state and local governments do not collect. At that individual's death the feds will line up, hands out demanding 35% of whatever the individual chose to bequeath. The opponents shout, "Double taxation! The individual paid taxes on his income when alive. His bequest is what was left over..."

The proponents scream, "The individual isn't paying anything; he's dead." Pretty lame, IMO.

Then there is the silly argument that if the "Rich" are allowed to keep the same amount of income as proposed by extending the current marginal rates, it will increase the federal deficit. To me, that's a clever play on words a lot of good folks are buying into it. <u>The federal deficit can only increase when the government spends more than it takes in during a given fiscal period.</u> It's much like overdrawing your checking account, writing checks without sufficient funds. The

feds can get away with it. Keeping more of your own after tax income does not add to any deficit!

Thanks for your time, Jaq

December 16, 2010

EDITOR: Viewpoint/Speak Out

by J. Wright

Remember when the liberal Democrats and their cohorts in the out-of-step media railed at former Alaska Governor Sarah Palin when she coined the term "Death Panels" in accusing the Obamacare plan of potential care rationing? Seems like she was spot on after all.

If you, a family member or close friend are a cancer victim right now, the chances of receiving the necessary drug treatment care needed may be in jeopardy, that according to this report recently filed by: http://biggovernment.com/capitolconfidential

From their article, "Sources on Capitol Hill have informed Capitol Confidential that the Food and Drug Administration (FDA) will indeed begin rationing late-stage cancer drugs. The FDA will make an 11am (EDT) announcement that it will begin denying Avastin to breast cancer patients but will graciously offer the creator of the drug a final show trial of a hearing in 60 days.

"The FDA will be judge, jury and executioner. Unfortunately, the victims of breast cancer will be the ones punished and harmed. The FDA has never before limited access to a drug based upon cost considerations. Yet there are some within the agency that are intent on breaking new ground to justify a rationing regime designed to drive down the cost of health care. Avastin is the test case. There is no evidence that the pending show trial will temper their enthusiasm for this rationing scheme.

Unbelievable. The FDA operates today under the auspices of the Obama Administration, an administration comprised of mostly intellectual leftist liberals who have taken over a once proud political party that used to defend "the little guy". Remember that term? Not today it seems. As it once was in Nazi Germany and later the USSR, seniors and the afflicted are expendable. How is that "Hope and Change" working now? Thanks for your time,

Thanks for your time, Jaq

December 29, 2010

<u>EDITOR: Viewpoint/SpeakOut</u>

by J. Wright

I recently submitted a letter to Viewpoint stating that the Food and Drug Administration (FDA) was going to remove Avastin, a cancer-treating drug, from the market. Another reader recently suggested that Avastin was not therapeutic and the FDA's action was not cost related.

The reader also recommended that before becoming alarmed, concerned individuals should research the facts first by using our computers, or if we didn't have a computer, visit the local library.

OK, upon rereading my original letter printed here, including the following URL: http://biggovernment.com/capitolconfidential that I had discovered whilst researching on my own computer.

I included it as an informational source stating; 'if you, a family member or close friend are a cancer victim right now, the chances of receiving the necessary drug treatment care needed may be in jeopardy', that according to a report filed by biggovernment.com. *(No, I didn't specify breast cancer but the report did.)*

The report stated in part, "Sources on Capitol Hill have informed Capitol Confidential that the Food and Drug Administration (FDA) will indeed begin rationing late-stage cancer drugs. The FDA will make an 11:00 A.M. (EDT) announcement that it will begin denying Avastin to breast cancer patients but will graciously offer the creator of the drug a final show trial of a hearing in 60 days.

It continued: "The FDA will be judge, jury and executioner. Sadly, the victims of breast cancer will be the ones punished and harmed.

I don't have a dog in the Avastin controversy. My intent was to alert readers that possible "rationing" might be on the health care front as former Alaska Governor Sarah Palin had suggested earlier when she used the term "Death Panels."

Thanks for your time, Jaq

Jaq's Note to readers: This is probably where I stopped slamming my head against my desktop. Constantly complaining 'to the choir' is not one of my life's last ambitions so I began to limit quietly my political 'outbursts.'

Instead, I went back to the revising and rewriting my initial eBook titled, A Scent of Suspicion, the first of four in a series of detective-fiction novels now available at the Createspace eStore/books.com and on Amazon.com/books.

Many of the letters and blogs that follow were also submitted and published nationally at Blogs Lucianne Loves, a part of the conservative web site, Lucianne.com.

2011

January 11, 2011
EDITOR: Viewpoint/Speak Out
by J. Wright

A lot has been discussed recently about the existence or not of "Death Panels" included in the Affordable Health Care Act (aka Obamacare).

According to an article titled <u>Death Panels are back, and that's good news!</u> taken from the San Jose Mercury News and published in Viewpoint on December 30. No, you won't probably find 'Death Panels' mentioned in any recent health care legislation; the lawmakers curiously rejected the idea.

Following passage of the bill, another Obama Administration unelected bureaucrat added a regulation that took effect after January 1st, which will now pay doctors to do what most doctors and accredited medical providers and hospitals have been doing for years as a service; to advise patients on end-of-life care, including options for advance directives on how they want to be treated. I call mine a Living Will.

My beef is that now our federal government is again micro managing an area of our lives that isn't broken… and paying for services that once were assumed. Like the feds have all of that spare money to spread around.

This is becoming a habit. Recently the FCC and it's five member appointed commission led by Democrats voted 3-2 to assume control of the Internet. This was attempted once before and the elected lawmakers rejected the idea. Add to that, a federal circuit judge deemed it unconstitutional. No matter, the FCC plowed ahead anyway ignoring Congress and the courts and announced that they were in control.

What's wrong with the Internet that it needs federal oversight and control? Nothing that I'm aware of, it works fine for me. The FCC says, yes, but something may come up later that needs our assistance. Fancy. To me this reeks of ruling, not governing, and by fiat or edict. I'll call it what it looks like: creeping dictatorship.

Thanks for your time, Jaq

January 18, 2011

EDITOR: Viewpoint/Speak Out

by J. Wright

I recently wrote decrying the Obama Administration's penchant for ruling by decree, avoiding the duly elected representatives will and allowing appointed bureaucrats to determine governmental policy. Here they go again.

Last Friday, President Obama's National Labor Relations Board *(NLRB)* announced plans to sue the states of Arizona, South Carolina, South Dakota, and Utah to allow unions to continue organizing through an open, signed, card-check process instead of the secret ballot. This is a fight Republicans should welcome, if they have the spine, because its terms and tactics reveal a White House desperate to bypass the will of the people yet again and rule by federal decree through appointed bureaucrats.

In November, voters in four states overwhelmingly approved state constitutional amendments that gave all employees the right to a secret ballot election when deciding whether to unionize. *(Secret ballot voting is a sacrosanct American tradition if you aren't already aware.)* The various state elections were blowouts that set back the labor cause. Voters approved the measures by 60 percent in Utah; 61

percent in Arizona; 79 percent in South Dakota and 86 percent in South Carolina.

Those huge percentages represent the will of the people; "We the People." But again, no matter, our President and his unelected bureaucrats seem to know better what's good for us than many of us, the "unwashed," do ourselves. Once again they will attempt to circumvent by federal regulation, the people's will. In doing so, the Obama Administration will bring suit against four sovereign states in order to appease and receive favor from the labor unions, unions that donate millions of campaign dollars to the Democrat Party.

Isn't that peachy?

In one of my previous postings here, I suggested it was like a "creeping dictatorship." How long will the American voters allow this behavior to continue?

Thanks for your time, Jaq

January 22, 2011
EDITOR: Viewpoint/Speak Out
by J. Wright

Previously I wrote where the Obama Administration's National Labor Relations Board (NLRB) had announced plans to sue the states of Arizona, South Carolina, South Dakota, and Utah to allow unions to continue organizing through an open, signed, card-check process instead of the secret ballot.

Well, dear readers, the NLRB has stepped up it's actions. The Daily Caller.com had this to say last Saturday: "President Barack Obama's administration continues its private sector unionization efforts, this time with the historically 'politically neutral' National Labor Relations Board. A newly proposed rule from the NLRB would require private sector companies to post employees' rights under the National Labor Relations Act, the legislation that gives employees the 'right' to unionize, in their workplaces.

"Former Department of Labor Solicitor Greg Jacob during the Bush Administration told The Daily Caller these unionization efforts are a misuse of the NLRB's power, especially because there is no legal basis whatsoever for what that board is trying to do." (Snip) "The National Labor Relations Board has always been neutral in these issues. At this point, now, they're trying to mandate employers post a posting in favor of unions."

Greg Jacob said he doesn't expect the NLRB to actually listen to any proposed public comments. He added, "... the NLRB went into this on a very, very shaky legal foundation at best, and that it's pretty clear NLRB members are more interested in their pro-union agenda than in upholding the law."

So again, a federal agency consisting of appointed bureaucrats assume dictatorial power, employ measures via rules or regulations of their own making, and blatantly ignore the law. At some point soon, this type of scurrilous behavior must be reined in. As I also mentioned earlier, it will take some lawmakers with the spine to do it.

Thanks for your time, Jaq

January 28, 2011

EDITOR: Viewpoint/Speak Out

by J. Wright

Allow me to plagiarize former President Ronald Reagan by posting his famous words, "Well, there they go again…"

In President Obama's recent State of the Union speech he brought up the proposal to "invest" *(spend taxpayer dollars)* on infrastructure projects: roads, bridges, etc. in order to create thousands, maybe hundreds of thousands of new jobs.

Hey! I'm all for anything that will create new private sector jobs, but haven't we heard this 'shovel-ready' bullshit before? I mean the fact that rebuilding questionable bridges and repairing the nation's roads would create new jobs? As I recall it was a highly advertised mainstay of the "American Recovery and Reinvestment Act," better known as the Obama Stimulus program.

I remember before its passing into law that I had a conversation with my liberal Minister regarding just how little of the $787 billions of dollars the stimulus bill would be spent on "infrastructure."

Incredibly it was about 4.1% of the total. My liberal minister, bless his soul, didn't agree with me. I turned out to be accurate, and didn't we all get to see those nice new signs plastered on the roadsides telling us where some of our tax dollars were going?

Most of the stimulus was spent on "saving jobs," much of it going to states to prop up their civil servant employees' wages, many union types by the way, but for only one year. Today we see state after state wondering what they are going to do now in order to make financial ends meet. No more stimulus this go-round, huh?

So President Obama is 'going to the well' again to promote national infrastructure repairs in order to create new jobs. Even to supporting a high-speed rail system as proposed by Democrat Senate Majority

Leader, Harry Reid, between Las Vegas and Los Angeles. Does Amtrak funding ring a discordant bell for you?

Thanks for your time, Jaq

January 30. 2011
EDITOR: Viewpoint/Speak Out
by J. Wright

Last year it was reported that the Department of Health and Human Resources (HHS) had granted 111 waivers to protect a few entities from the onerous regulations of the new national health care overhaul, titled The Patient Protection and Affordable Health Care Act, aka Obamacare.

Dr. Milton R. Wolf, a board-certified diagnostic radiologist, medical director, and a cousin of President Barack Obama, wrote in the Washingtontimes.com on January 25, 2011: "That number quickly and quietly climbed to 222, and last week we learned that the number of Obamacare privileged 'escapees' has skyrocketed to 733."

"Among the fortunate is a who's who list of unions, businesses and even several cities and four states *(Massachusetts, New Jersey, Ohio and Tennessee)* but none of the friends of Barack feature as prominently as the Service Employees International Union *(SEIU)*.

"How can you get your own free pass from Obamacare? Maybe you can just donate $27 million to President Obama's campaign efforts. That's what SEIU did in 2008. Frankly, many of us will face increased health insurance premiums, but special interests like the unions will not."

It was President Obama himself who infamously said, on October 25, 2010, "We're gonna punish our enemies and we're gonna reward our friends *(who stand with us on issues that are important to us.)*"

Apparently he looks at many of us as being "enemies." How pitiful. The 14th amendment of the U.S. Constitution clearly prohibits states from denying any person within its jurisdiction the equal protection of the laws. Shouldn't that amendment also apply to President Obama and Obamacare?

Thanks for your time, Jaq

February 21, 2011

<u>EDITOR: Viewpoint/Speak Out</u>

by J. Wright

Damian Paletta of the Wall Street Journal writes from Paris: U.S. Treasury Secretary Timothy Geithner said Saturday that the package of spending cuts the (Republican led) House of Representatives passed earlier in the day would "undermine and damage our capacity to create jobs and expand the economy."

Secretary Geithner went on to say, "The House of Representatives early Saturday voted 235-189 to cut more than $61 billion from current spending levels, a move considered to be the biggest one-time cut in budget history if enacted. Senate Democrats are poised to reject the measure, and prospects for a government shutdown could grow if an agreement isn't reached by March 4."

So, if Harry Reid's Democrats reject the proposal and the government is shut down, somehow it's the fault of the Republicans. So far, I haven't seen many Democrats in favor of cutting anything, even a little bit. This proposal takes care of <u>last year's business</u>, business the House Democrats intentionally ignored for political reasons prior to the fall elections. They refused to pass a budget in order to save seats; it didn't work.

Mr. Geithner pointed to the package of spending cuts and new spending programs the White House detailed in its (President Obama's) budget proposal several days ago as the best way to both reduce deficits while still investing in economic growth.

"Investing?" Let's call it what it is; more government spending and more taxes. This is the same administration that just celebrated its second anniversary of the "Stimulus Bill" that promised to hold unemployment under 8%. We know how that worked. Why should we believe President Obama's proposed budget is the answer? Nothing he has suggested has worked so far. And why are the Republicans going to be the fall guys if the Senate Democrats reject a proposed cost cutting measure?

Thanks for your time, Jaq

March 8, 2011

EDITOR: Viewpoint/Speak Out
by J. Wright

Can any of us afford to spend 20-cents less from every $100 in our personal budget? Inexplicably the Democrat led U.S. Senate says it can't ... it would be "Draconian!"

Draconian? I find that unimaginable.

The House Republicans have passed a $61 billion budget cut *(or 1 & 6/10%, $4 billion of which has passed the Senate in a recent continuing resolution)*. The Democrat led Senate has now proposed a cut of a mere $8.7 billion, *(2/10%)* when the Congressional Budget Office analysis is taken into account. To others and me, these figures would be considered "rounding errors" in most accounting practices when discussing this amount of money. Not in Washington, D.C. where even lowering a proposed increase is considered a "Cut". *(Face it, we're doomed.)*

If you had a $100 weekly grocery budget, the Republican plan would have you spending $1.60 less per week. The Democrat plan would have you spending 20-cents less. LOL!

Again, this is truly unimaginable that either party can't justify more real savings. I guess the message sent via the results of the November election didn't sink in, and it's not their money they are dealing with anyway. So what?

Suggestion? Write, don't email or call, Michigan's Democrat Senators Levin and Stabenow and remind them *(as if they care)* the nation is on the brink of bankruptcy, unless you don't give a rip as apparently they don't.

Thanks for your time, Jaq

April 29, 2011
EDITOR: Viewpoint/Speak Out
by J. Wright

The arrogance of our federal governmental agencies in their continuing quest to retain power, regardless of impending job losses, is overwhelming. If you enjoy paying $4.00 or more per gallon for gasoline and you blindly support President Obamas suggestion that the Saudis should be producing more oil for our consumption, stop reading right now. This piece wouldn't interest you.

Taken from http://pearce.house.gov, Roswell, NM (April 28, 2011)

"An estimated 750 New Mexico residents attended a rally tonight in Roswell to oppose the listing of the Dunes Sagebrush Lizard as an endangered species. The listing threatens to have a devastating effect on the thousands of oil and gas related jobs in New Mexico."

Like the Pacific NW's Spotted Owl, the California Snail Darter and Sand Flea (*orchestoidea californiana*) among others, the Dunes Sagebrush Lizard addition to the growing list as an endangered species will cost possibly 20,000 oil and gas jobs in New Mexico alone. When the Federal Fish and Wildlife Service was asked if they had taken into consideration the potential job loss, they brushed it off as incidental.

Congressman Steven Pearce, R-NM says, "My office has asked for data from Fish and Wildlife on how jobs will be impacted, and they claim they don't have the information."

The only way to determine if any New Mexico Dunes Sagebrush Lizard is endangered or not is to carefully place it on its back and 'count the scales located on its front legs between the armpit and the elbow'.

A lizard with five scales is NOT endangered. One with four scales is ... yet no DNA tests have determined if the two identical lizards are the same species, just bureaucratic scale counting resulting in potentially massive job losses. Seriously?

This is definitely "Change." The same as the fresh water that supplied California food farms until it was shut off because of the endangered minnow sized Delta Smelt Fish.

Thanks for your time, Jaq

Thursday, June 2, 2011

When is a Lie the Truth?

by J. Wright

It's amazing the things one can discover from listening to a few minutes of talk radio, or watching a sane TV news broadcast ... certainly little the famed Mainstream Media cares to divulge.

I "learned" today that our president, Barack H. Obama, truly believes that our current federal income tax rates are the lowest in recent history, lower even than the Ronald W. Reagan era, and in his opinion it's only 'fair' to raise income taxes on couples making more than $250,000, or individuals making more than $200,000 annually. This he told the astonished Republican leaders who met with him earlier this week at the White House.

While most of the Republicans present rolled their eyes at this assertion regarding Reagan's tax rates, it was explained to the president that Reagan era rates were actually lower. What is different today are the loopholes in place that Reagan previously abolished. What is also true is that tax revenues today ARE LOWER than in the Reagan era, when all factors are taken into consideration.

In explanation, House Majority Whip Kevin McCarthy (R-CA) was quick to counter the president's claim on low tax rates, saying, "...actually, our corporate tax rates are the highest in the world." President Obama acknowledged that U.S. corporate tax rates are higher than most other nations.

Rep. Steve Scalise (R-LA) explained "...that's a big deal. The high rates hurt American competitiveness and job creation - so the folks that are trying to earn money, get a job, so they can pay that 'low tax rate,' they can't even do that right now because we aren't competitive with the rest of the world." (Why do Liberals insist on making taxes punitive, like somehow ignoring that a business must maintain its profit margin or go bust, and by doing so, it passes additional operating expenses *(taxes)* on to the general public?)

It was reported too, that President Obama is not interested in slowing or lowering the incessant government spending now in place, rather he wants more money to spend, ergo the request for an additional $2 trillion to be added to our national debt limit. With that, recall that two weeks ago he requested a "clean up or down vote" on raising the debt limit. The Republican led House gave it to him a day ago and it lost big time. Some eighty-two (82) Democrats voted 'No' including Nancy Pelosi. Afterward the White House and the Democrat leaders claimed the vote was a fraud, a joke; that after giving them what President Obama had asked for.

One radio news commentator used the expression, "You give me that apple and I'll let you paint the fence white." Too damn funny IMO.

Later, on the Neil Cavuto FOX News financial program, Cavuto exchanged views on the current jobless rate with a Democrat House member from California who repeated several times that in order to keep our economy "growing" we must maintain the same fiscal policies that have given us a net gain of 125 million new jobs under Obama.

Cavuto countered saying that they has been <u>NO</u> net gain in jobs. The Democrat kept smiling and maintained that Neil was wrong. What is true, Cavuto's staff, *(along with Roger Hedgecock's of <u>Conservative Talk Radio</u> using government stats available on line)* found that under Obama, since January of 2009, the country has suffered a net <u>LOSS of 2.5 million jobs</u>; a 3.75 million swing from what the Democrat politician falsely claimed. My question: who is the propagandist who informs these people?

A few weeks ago, Cavuto had a similar exchange with an Obama supporter who maintained over and over that thirty-one (31) new drilling permits had been issued for the Gulf of Mexico since the BP spill, Cavuto said "No, only three (3) have been issued."

Cavuto was proven right. *(Again using stats gleaned from .gov web sites.)* My question remains; who is the propagandist who informs these people? Or is it their practice to lie, keep lying, and maybe convince enough folks that a lie is an actual fact?

If the financial crisis, that caused this ongoing recession, was brought about under President George W. Bush, it's also true that this "recovery" *(or lack of same)* belongs to Obama. It ain't working.

Thanks for your time, Jaq

Monday, June 20, 2011

HAS THE GOVERNMENT STOLEN YOUR IDENTITY?

by J. Wright

Readers, please bear with me whilst I indulge in some uncharacteristic make believe.

Imagine that when your next credit card bill arrives, you open it and discover that you, your wife and two kids suddenly owe $180,000 more than you thought.

"This is not right!" you say and immediately get on the telephone and call your credit card company.

You get a responsible individual on the line and ask, "What's the meaning of this $180,000 balance in new charges that I didn't make?"

"Oh…" the individual responds, "those aren't new charges, this has

been going on for a number of years but we never showed it on your billings. Your Uncle made those charges. He has control of your account too.

"What? Which Uncle?"

"Sam, your Uncle Sam. He indicated that he had control of your family's credit card account and he needed to use it to help some folks who are disadvantaged and to promote some of his favorite projects."

"You must be kidding! I never gave him that kind of control!"

"Yes, you did. A long time ago."

"That's unbelievable. So what is he doing with our money?"

"Well … unfortunately, he mishandles and wastes a lot of it. A lot goes to people who are out of work, or simply lazy, or ill, or dying. A lot of it he spends on himself too, but he hides that from our prying eyes. He says those folks he is helping don't have a credit card so he uses your money. He says, 'It's only fair and you can afford it'."

"I can't believe this. How am I ever going to pay this off, or is he going to pay it off?"

"Unfortunately, your Uncle doesn't have any money of his own; he has to use yours. You can't pay it off either so your Uncle will continue to keep charging to your account. He suggested to us that you could take a second job in order to make more money available to him. Even now he is asking for an increase in your credit limit and we have to give it to him. "

"Why?"

"Because we always have and it appears now that we don't have a choice."

"Well, if I can't ever pay this balance off, who will?"

"Your children will become responsible for the balance, along with their children, and their children and their children … unfortunately it's a never ending cycle."

"Isn't there some way to end it?"

"Sure, if you can find enough people willing to replace your respective Uncles. Everyone is in the same predicament; all of you have a spendthrift Uncle Sam."

"And if we can't?"

"Then you live with the fact that you and your children's children will be in debt to us forever, and not just the $45,000 each that everyone in your household owes today. Your Uncle has made promises to a lot of people, financial promises that are as yet unpaid amounting to tens of thousands of dollars; about a half million dollars more that you and every other family are responsible for, okay?"

"Okay? You must be kidding."

... ...

So, what if you did wake up one day and discover yourself in that financial mess?

The reality is, you don't need to wake up; you are already there. The reality is our National Debt has surpassed $14,440,900,000,000.00 and is growing *(that's about $46,000+ for every man, woman and child)*. Our annual government expense will exceed our revenues this year by more than $1.381 trillion and growing and eventually added to the National Debt.

Add to that the Unfunded Mandates as reported recently; promises made by our government to seniors, veterans, the disadvantaged, etc. that stand at a whopping $61.6 trillion.

Do you agree that it may be past time to replace Uncle and get the borrowing and spending under control?

Thanks for your time, Jaq

Prodigious Political Ponderings & Prognostications...

June 17, 2011

EDITOR: Viewpoint/Speak Out

by J. Wright

In a recent posting, a fellow Cadillac News Viewpoint contributor
extolled the virtues of isolated examples of socialism, i.e. credit
unions, cooperatives, and municipal owned utility companies, etc.

As a form of government, socialism is a failure: it doesn't work. A
socialist totalitarian central government makes decisions affecting
the lives of the entire population, a population that because of
socialism, owns nothing of its own. In a nutshell, socialism is rather
a poor middle ground between free market capitalism and
communism. The government controls most production and
distribution, or the way foundations are run. As with Medicaid or
Social Security: citizens pay but the government has total control of
the distribution.

Socialism didn't work for the collective minded settlers in the
Jamestown Colony; they were dying in droves until the principle of
"free enterprise" allowed individuals their own property on which to
plant, harvest and sell crops. This was the beginning of the free
enterprise system that made America a once great nation.

Fast forwarding in world history, Benito Mussolini's Socialist Italy,
pre-WW II, was wildly acclaimed by the European and western
elitist academia and liberal leftists as "Nirvana, the government of
the future!" We know how that ended. Certainly, Mussolini found
out.

Today many modern day socialist countries are going bankrupt
as quickly as the United States. Our financial problems stem mostly
from ponzi like federal entitlement social schemes that consistently
spend more in benefits than they collect in revenues; i.e., Medicare,

Medicaid, to name a couple. I intentionally left out Social Security, whose financial plight is as horrendous as the others are, because the reader didn't consider it to be an "entitlement." Call it whatever, it is fast going broke too.

Is socialism the answer? Maybe as with red wine: in moderation in some isolated cases, but as a form of central government? No way. Unless you choose to follow Cuba's sterling example. Thanks for your time,

Thanks for your time, Jaq

June 20, 2011 –

EDITOR: Viewpoint/Speak Out

by J. Wright

Adolph Hitler's Minister of 'Mis-Information', Josef Goebbels, theorized that if people are subjected to a faulty statement *(a lie)* often enough, eventually it becomes accepted as truth.

I read here recently that major oil companies pay no federal taxes. The contributor must have our major oil companies confused with General Electric based on a prevailing argument whether corporate giant GE paid any federal taxes last year, or if they instead, received a $3.2 billion refund ... the financial experts are still at each other's throats with that mess.

Investor's Business Daily says this about major oil companies; *(http://seekingalpha.com/article/78793-oil-companies-paid-more-than-bottom-75-of-taxpayers)* "...according to the American Petroleum Institute, in 2006 alone, U.S. oil companies paid some $138 billion in taxes to the Internal Revenue Service [IRS], and that doesn't include special oil severance, sales and use taxes companies also had to pay."

An Internal Revenue Service .pdf file states: "...in 2005 *(the most recent year for which data are available)*, the bottom 75% of all individual taxpayers *(about 100 million taxpayers out of 132 million total)* paid about $130.9 billion in income taxes."

That's $4+ billion less than the oil companies paid. This fact gets lost.

Major corporations hire the best tax lawyers available to utilize the tax loopholes our elected Democrat and Republican Congressmen and Senators write into the ever-growing federal tax code. Some of these same corporate tax lawyers once worked for the United States government and designed that tax code. No wonder they can find the areas that favor their new employers.

Today, the poor do not pay taxes to the federal government, many receive money back; it's called an 'Earned Income Tax Credit'. *(Call it welfare too ... nothing ventured, much gained.)* Perhaps your family qualifies?

To find out visit:
http://www.irs.gov/individuals/article/0,,id=96406,00.html

Until our antiquated taxation system is changed, where some pay nothing and get paid for it, there will be inequities, and all perfectly legal.

Thanks for your time, Jaq

June 22, 2011 –

EDITOR: Viewpoint/Speak Out

by J. Wright

I read in a recent Cadillac News Viewpoint contribution that, "…in Clinton's presidency, income taxes were raised."

Yes, they were raised, and retroactively too, after he'd campaigned non-stop on a "middle-class tax cut." I'm still awaiting mine. Do you suppose candidate Clinton duped us?

Then I read, "Clinton's last two years in office saw budget surpluses of $500 billion*." (I question that amount, but those last years had a Republican House of Representatives in control of the federal purse strings.)*

On February 2, 1999, the NY Times quoted Speaker Dennis Hastert, R-Illinois, as saying, "The president's budget ambitiously spends almost every cent of the surplus on Washington based programs not set aside for Social Security reform. Clearly, the president sees the surplus as an opportunity to expand the power, the influence and the size of the federal government." Some things never change.

So did those "Clinton Surpluses" come from higher taxes? Not exactly. Clinton's surpluses were partly a result of the Republican's austere 'Contract With America,' and the so-called 'Peace Dividend' *(huge Defense Department budgetary cuts), the* Social Security tax on payrolls, and the treasury being substantially fattened by incoming receipts from the previously bailed out Savings and Loan associations; funds that Republican President Reagan had previously ordered returned to the taxpayers.

That's part of "the rest of the story." Giving Clinton some credit, the National Debt showed a marginal increase of only a few billion dollars in his last year in office as opposed the "normal" mega billion dollar increases we are now getting used to. So much for budget surpluses. Based on past results, when sane Republican adults control the nation's purse strings, fiscal responsibility can happen, not always as we witnessed in Bush 43's last two years, but it's possible. Lastly, if Warren Buffet's secretary's wages were taxed on capital gains income rates as the majority of Warren's are, her tax bill would be lower.

Thanks for your time, Jaq

Thursday, July 21, 2011

"Cleaning up George W. Bush's Mess…"

by J. Wright

"Cleaning up Bush's mess…" I'm amazed how President G. W. Bush continues to be cast as the spendthrift by the loyal opposition: it's always "Bush's fault." Yes, the National Debt increased substantially during Bush's terms in office, especially during his last two years with <u>Democrats Nancy Pelosi and Harry Reid in charge of the purse strings</u>.

The Wall Street Journal, October 5, 2007, reported: "The Congressional Budget Office estimated that the U.S. federal budget deficit for fiscal year 2007, which ended Sunday, was about $161 billion. That's down from the $248 billion shortfall recorded in fiscal 2006." Bush's 2008 deficit was $239 Billion. This year's (2011) projected deficit is $1.65 Trillion, <u>close to six times higher than 2008</u>.

From the same article: "While annual federal spending grew 2.8% in fiscal 2007 over fiscal 2006, year to year, revenue grew 6.7%. Individual income-tax receipts are estimated to be 11.3% higher than last year, and corporate income tax receipts are estimated to be 5% higher."

That's some difference in total annual deficits and growth rates in comparison to what we have experienced in the past two and one-half years under President Obama and his economic 'advisors' *(most of whom have recently left for greener pastures)*. Discontent and uncertainty are the only things that have grown lately.

Compare the Obama Administration's deficit for the single month of February 2011 when it reached a record setting $223 billion to the fiscal year deficit of $239 billion recorded in 2008. *(Whoa!)*

United States Treasury Department web site figures show that Bush and Congress increased the National Debt about $4.97 trillion with it topping off at $10.7 trillion when Obama assumed office. Today the National Debt is hovering at $14.5 trillion. Do the math. That's an unsustainable increase of $3.8 trillion in two and one-half years of spending compared to Bush's $4.97 trillion in eight.

To make the math even simpler: during Bill Clinton's presidency the nation's indebtedness increased at $547 Million daily. Under President George W. Bush the debt skyrocketed to $1.6 billion daily. During President Obama's term it has gone totally ballistic at a rate of $4.6 billion per day increase.

If President Obama is "…cleaning up Bush's mess," I would suggest he is well on his way to making a greater mess of his own on the backs of future struggling taxpayers and foreign lenders.

Thanks for your time, Jaq

Sunday, July 31, 2011

Putting Principles and Country Before Political Party?

by J. Wright

Conservative journalist Jennifer Rubin posted in the Washington post.com on Sunday, July 31, 2011: "We are on the verge, it seems, of a deal on the debt-ceiling that would embody two essential goals of the Tea Party and the GOP more generally: no new tax revenues and significant spending cuts equal to or greater than the size of the debt-ceiling increase."

Wikipedia.com describes The Tea Party as "…an American populist political movement that is generally recognized as conservative and libertarian, and has sponsored protests and supported political candidates since 2009. It endorses reduced government spending, opposition to taxing in varying degrees, reduction of the National Debt and federal budget deficit, and adherence to an originality interpretation of the United States Constitution."

That's novel and personally, I find it refreshing. But not Martin Frost, former Democrat representative from Texas. In a recent politico.com article, Frost likens the Tea Party to the "Taliban." So … if you don't agree with something, label it with a bad name?

It goes on: NYT Liberal columnist Tom Friedman is quoted by jewschool.com saying: "Alas, that is the Tea Party … If the sane Republicans do not stand up to this *Hezbollah* faction in their midst, the Tea Party will take the G.O.P. on a suicide mission."

Nicholas Kristof, who wrote in last Sunday's New York Times, is a liberal columnists posted in Media Research .org, "…an edgy argument to denigrate the risk of terrorism in favor of their beef of the week: 'Republican, Zealots, and Our Security.' Kristoff actually likened the danger posed by Tea Party sympathizers in Congress (domestic zealots) to Al Qaeda."

Would the alleged "Danger posed" be the fact that the Tea Partiers in this Congress aren't particularly concerned if they are reelected or not? I find that refreshing too: they put principles and country before party, and that seems to terrify the liberal socialists in our elected bodies and media.

Thanks for your time, Jaq

Monday, September 5, 2011

<u>Are the Democrats Becoming Unstrung?</u>

by J. Wright

Not long ago we heard Democrat vice-president Joe Biden liken Tea Partiers to *"terrorists."*

Then later, Representative Maxine Waters, D-CA, suggested that *"...the Tea Party can go to Hell!"*

Following that, Democrat Representative Frederica Wilson, D-FL, at a Town Hall meeting in Miami sponsored by the Congressional Black Caucus (CBC) said, *"The real enemy is the Tea Party!"*

Last week, Representative Andre Carson, D-IN, at another CBC meeting in Miami said, *"...that some in Congress would love to see us as second-class citizens and some of them in Congress right now of this tea party movement would love to see you and me... hanging on a tree."*

Now today, Labor Day 2011 in Detroit, Michigan, Teamster Union boss Jimmy Hoffa had this to say when introducing the president of the United States, Barack H. Obama, as posted verbatim from <u>realclearpolitics.com</u>:

Teamsters President Jimmy Hoffa had some profane, combative words for Republicans while warming up the crowd for President Obama in Detroit, Michigan on Monday.

"We got to keep an eye on the battle that we face: The war on workers. And you see it everywhere, it is the Tea Party. And you know, there is only one way to beat and win that war. The one thing about working people is we like a good fight. And you know what? They've got a war, they got a war with us and there's only going to be one winner. It's going to be the workers of Michigan, and America. We're going to win that war," Jimmy Hoffa Jr. said to a heavily union crowd.

"President Obama, this is your army. We are ready to march. Let's take these sons-of-bitches out and give America back to an America where we belong," Hoffa added.

So now Mr. Hoffa, in introducing Detroit's guest, Barack H. Obama, the president of the United States of America, forgot that he wasn't in a union hall full of loyal, or somewhat loyal supporters, and he resorted to gutter language profanity; cuss words that have declared war on American citizens whose purpose in life is for <u>lower taxes, smaller government, cutting government spending and essentially giving the country back to its citizens</u>. Do you see anything wrong with Hoffa's picture?

How frightening it must be for Jimmy Hoffa, Joe Biden, Maxine Waters, Frederica Wilson and Andre Carson. Apparently, if their words make their case, this Tea Party movement is something to really fear, and it appears to me that a lot of high level Democrats are becoming unstrung because of it.

I don't normally make suggestions to Democrats, Liberals, Socialists, Marxists and Communists, etc. *(First, how do you separate them?)* Anyway, to mix a metaphor or two, I'd strongly suggest they not kick sand in the face of a sleeping giant.

The Tea Partiers I'm acquainted with probably will not take lightly being called "sons-of-bitches," a term more suited for General Patton when describing the NAZIs among other things, and the end result might be more frightening then what their liberal adversaries perceive today.

Thanks for your time, Jaq

February 2, 2012

EDITOR: Viewpoint/Speak Out
by J. Wright

I read in a recent contribution to Viewpoint, "Sadly, the current tax structure favors the 1 percent to continue increasing their share of the nation's income and wealth."

I agree that the 1%ers wealth will increase; it's unavoidable considering the vast Quantitative Easing created by the Federal Reserve now feeding the DJI averages. I also agree with President Obama in a way.

On the campaign trail he suggests that everybody should be "paying their fair share," except he would possibly exclude the 49.5% of the country that pay no federal income tax whatsoever.

I think all of us should "have some skin in the game," to me, that would be fair.

The contributor wrote how the top 1% has made huge financial gains since the 1970s, apparently, as he assumes, at the expense of the remaining 99%. Does that mean if I don't clean up my plate and waste food that some disadvantaged third world individual will starve? I think it means that someone may have taken some financial risks and in doing so they made more money than their employees. It's called capitalism. It's not a perfect economic system but compared to the alternatives it's the best, except for possibly the current federal tax structure Folks find it popular to blame presidents for the massive spending and national debt. Actually, it's the legislators whom we elect that are in charge of the purse strings.

Since the 1970s Democrats have controlled the House, except for 12 years between 1995 and 2007 and 6 years of George W. Bush's presidency. The Democrats controlled the Senate except between 1983 and 1987 and again between 1997 and 2001. If you care to complain about the current tax structure, contact your Senator or Congressman, they write the tax code. Many fall into that 1%.

Thanks for your time, Jaq

Sunday, July 1, 2012

Is Fast & Furious a "Racist Witch Hunt" or a Cover-up?

by J. Wright

Much has been written and broadcast of late concerning the botched Fast and Furious gun-walking program reinstated by the Obama administration after a "sting" program to track guns crossing the Mexican border was canceled in 2007 by the George W. Bush administration because of the inability to trace those weapons. In 2009, Secretary of State Hillary Clinton 'patriotically' stated that most of the illegal weapons in the hands of Mexican drug cartels came from the United States.

Later, someone in one of the law enforcement agencies of our government initiated 'Fast and Furious'. To date, we don't know who initiated it. No one has been publicly forced to resign, or worse, brought to justice, the result? Two federal agents are dead, not to mention hundreds of Mexicans while many administration documents were questionably protected under Executive Privilege.

Townhall.com Editor/Journalist, Katie Pavlich, writes on page 145 of her book titled Fast and Furious, Barack Obama's Bloodiest Scandal and its Shameful Cover-up, *"The full consequences of Fast and Furious are not yet known. Emails released under congressional subpoena suggest that Attorney General Eric Holder, Homeland Security Secretary Janet Napolitano and their senior lieutenants were involved in devising and approving the program in 2009. Both Holder and Napolitano have made statements at odds with the facts. Holder has made statements at odds with his own testimony. As congressional investigators uncover more documents, what was initially a limited inquiry into one government program could*

---

become an investigation into perjury, obstruction of justice, and a government cover-up."

Former Speaker of the House Nancy Pelosi says this investigation is all about racism; an attack on Attorney General Holder. Other Democrats call it a "Witch Hunt." I disagree; if any racism is involved it's in ignoring the many Mexicans that are dead because of this program gone awry. Since when is uncovering an alleged crime a "Witch Hunt?" Maybe only in Pelosi's mind. Far-reaching programs as massive as this do not begin at the bottom and "trickle" up.

Sources:
www.youtube.com/watch?v=TWckd5P3Fuw
www.freerepublic.com/focus/f-news/2793192/posts
http://www.foxnews.com/politics/2012/06/26/as-campaign-heats-up-democrats-focus-on-racism/ Katie Pavlich's 2012 book titled "Fast and Furious," published by Regenery Publishing, Inc.

Thanks for your time, Jaq

October 8, 2012 –
EDITOR: Viewpoint/Speak Out
by J. Wright

We have heard over and over again from President Obama and vice-President Biden how "Bush's failed economic policies" caused the worst economic downturn since the Great Depression and that the Romney-Ryan Republicans want to take us back to those failed policies of deregulation and tax cuts for the wealthy. Next week in a Town Hall foreign policy debate setting we could hear it once again from the President.

If Romney would explain it as succinctly as FOX News Channel analyst Brit Hume did this week it would cut President Obama's argument off at the knees.

Hume explained first, the "Bush Tax Cuts" didn't lower taxes just for the rich; they lowered income tax rates <u>across the board</u>. The initial result was a shortening of the recession Bush "inherited" from President Clinton.

Second, federal revenues increased through 2007 and lowered the federal deficit for three of those years even with the cost of paying for 9/11 and two wars.

Third, the tax cuts had absolutely nothing to do with the 2008 housing market and mortgage loan collapse.

As for deregulation, Hume said, *"President Obama himself has said that former President Bush put more regulations in place than he has in the same time frame. It is true that there is one bit of deregulation regularly blamed by liberal economists for helping create the speculative bubble that led to the financial crisis and the great recession. That was the lifting of the legal barrier between commercial and investment banking. But that barrier was lifted in 1999 in a bill signed into law by President Bill Clinton."*

Will the Republican candidate Romney explain this in the same fashion in a debate with millions of voters watching? How can President Obama possibly refute the facts if Romney lays them out as simply as Brit Hume?

Thanks for your time, Jaq

Tuesday, October 29, 2013

How Obamacare Evolved...

by J. Wright

In June of 2009, I published a letter in our local newspaper's opinion column. In it I vigorously complained about the proposed cost of what has now been tabbed "Obamacare." It was only a proposal then; today it is a joke.

The following is a portion of that letter:

"President Obama is currently pushing for an omnibus healthcare reform package that originally was to top out at $1 trillion ($1,000,000,000,000.00) over ten years. The Congressional Budget Office (CBO) took a closer look and came up with $1.6 trillion."

Today, the revised figure is upwards of $3 trillion IF they intend to cover every American, or it will cost nothing at all (scoff) if you believe Senate Majority Leader Harry Reid. This astronomical amount of debt added to our grandchildren's increasing debt (Obama says we're broke) might provide Americans with a questionable healthcare system on a par with UK and Canada. Or not.

Why is this legislation being considered? To provide access or coverage for the unverified millions of Americans who for a multitude of reasons, some personal, don't have and don't want health insurance coverage, or is it another governmental power grab?" In 2009, the plan was advertised as necessary in order to provide insurance coverage for 30 million uninsured Americans. Last month it was reported that 30 million Americans would still not be covered. That begs an answer to the question; What was the point?

In 2009 I wrote often and long in opposition to Obamacare; I suggested we were being duped and I caught a ton of flak for that remark from loyal Obama supporters. Well, look at the results now that it is the law of the land. If you can honestly claim we weren't duped, then you're not one of those now saying, "I was for Obamacare until I had to pay for it."

Thanks for your time, Jaq

The following article rates an OMG!
This crap has me pulling my hair out by the roots.

Obama: "I'll Start Obeying the Law IF You Pass One I Like."

By Craig Bannister | November 22, 2014 1:08pm ET

Pres. Obama said today that he will begin respecting limits on his authority once Congress passes an immigration bill he likes.

In his weekly address, titled "Immigration Accountability Executive Action," Obama responded to those who criticize him for exceeding his authority by issuing an executive order changing immigration law:

"As you might have heard, there are Members of Congress who question my authority to make our immigration system work better. Well, I have one answer for that: Pass a bill. The day I sign it into law, the actions I've taken to help solve this problem will no longer be necessary."

So, his "one answer" to claims he lacks the authority appears to be that his actions are "necessary," even though he doesn't have the authority to take them.

And, if both Houses of Congress pass a bill saying that everyone who entered the country illegally must go – no "ands," "ifs," or "buts" – does this mean that Obama would sign, respect, and enforce it?

Obama also declared that his administration will focus enforcement on "people who are threats to our security":

"I took those actions this week. We're providing more resources at the border to help law enforcement personnel stop illegal crossings, and send home those who do cross over. We'll focus enforcement resources on people who are threats to our security -- felons, not families; criminals, not children. And we'll bring more undocumented immigrants out of the shadows so they can play bythe rules, pay their full share of taxes, pass a criminal background check, and get right with the law."

But, as the Washington Examiner points out, that does not include "drunk drivers, sex abusers, drug dealers, gun offenders."

~ ~ ~

And there it is, "part of the ugly, ongoing story", my friends. As I said, preaching to the choir was disheartening and hard on my hypertension. As a nation, I hope we can survive until Election Day of 2016.

Meanwhile, please check out my Detective Len Morgan Novels. Available at Createspace eStore and Amazon.com/books

A Scent of Suspicion
A Detective Len Morgan Novel #1

San Fernando Valley, California, circa 1996...

Veteran Homicide Lieutenant Len Morgan and his partner Jeff Robinson, of the Valley West Devonshire precinct, investigate the grizzly slaying of a local hooker. Their only significant clue is a faint scent of cologne lingering in her shabby hotel room.

One frustrating dead-end leads to another. Suddenly they are involved with the U.S. Treasury Department; the Russian Mafia; three slain fellow cops; a cagey international assassin; and a senseless classroom shooting.

His Father's Sons
A Detective Len Morgan Novel #2

San Fernando Valley, California, circa 1996...

Len Morgan, Valley West Police Department Homicide Captain, returns to work, following a two-week furlough spent sailing his sloop on the blue Pacific, and finds his department knee-deep in the investigation of a mysterious car explosion that left the victim charred beyond recognition. Len later gets word from his mother that his father, declared MIA in Korea 46 years earlier, has resurfaced and sent her a huge sum of money.

This leads Len to a bizarre reunion with his estranged father and his two Asian half-brothers, all of whom he learns are international criminals involved in a murderous and deceptive high-tech scheme to infiltrate and destroy our current system of government, and to cleverly frame a diabolical murder.

A Passion for Revenge
A Detective Len Morgan Novel #3

Circa July-August, 1996 - San Fernando Valley, California...

Newly retired from the Valley West Homicide unit, Len Morgan's attempt to become a Private Investigator gets off to a rocky beginning starting with the assassination of his longtime friend and new business partner, Fast Eddie. Subsequently, Len finds himself pursuing two adversaries, gangster Emilio Ramos and 'Lotus Blossom,' a female assassin, each wishing to kill off the other.

Ultimately, he rejoins the official investigative ranks at the Valley West Police Department in a newly formed Major Crimes Unit, teaming up with his former partner and long-time best friend, Jeff Robinson, along with two homicide detectives recently drafted from the LAPD Major Crimes force. This tale takes the reader to Vietnam, Colorado and southern Texas in a mad sequence of events, though seemingly unrelated, finally come together.

CHAOS...and Cops!
A Detective Len Morgan Novel #4

Circa September 1996 - San Fernando Valley, California...

Major Crimes Unit Lieutenant Detective Len Morgan's long-time partner, Jeff Robinson, is shot and hospitalized after interrupting a liquor store robbery that left two people dead, one by Robinson's weapon. Len teams up with a veteran homicide detective. Later, a firebombing destroys Robinson's house, followed the next day by the firebombing of the Devonshire Hills Police Precinct's favorite coffee shop, leaving several uniformed officers dead. In an effort to solve these bombings, other West Valley detectives are brought in "from the bench."

With Jeff Robinson out of the hospital, convalescing and deciding whether detective work is his "bag," Len gains a new, younger partner. They soon become involved with the Beverly Hills Police Department, the Los Angeles FBI Bureau and Interpol in an effort to chase down a pair of elusive murder suspects; one, a suspected Israeli Mossad agent gone rogue.

~ ~ ~

INSANIA INTERRUPTUS
A Detective Len Morgan Novel #5

Will be out in early summer, 2015.

www.ingramcontent.com/pod-product-compliance
Lightning Source LLC
Chambersburg PA
CBHW070354290526
45790CB00004B/1479